Better Homes and Gardens®

DINNER EXPRESS

WILEY

John Wiley & Sons, Inc.

For general information on our other products and services
or for technical support, please contact our Customer Care
Department within the United States at (800) 762–2974, outside
the United States at (317) 572–3993 or fax (317) 572–4002.

Wiley also publishes its books in a variety of electronic
formats. Some content that appears in print may not be
available in electronic books. For more information about
Wiley products, visit our web site at www.wiley.com.

Library of Congress Cataloging-in-Publication Data is available
upon request.

ISBN: 978-0470-54029-9

Printed in the United States of America

10 9 8 7 6 5 4 3 2 1

Cover photo: Chicken and Pasta in Peanut Sauce, page 24

Meredith Corporation

Editors: Jan Miller; Lisa Kingsley, Waterbury Publications, Inc.
Contributing Editor: Tricia Laning, Lois White, Waterbury Publications, Inc.

John Wiley & Sons, Inc.

Publisher: Natalie Chapman
Associate Publisher: Jessica Goodman
Executive Editor: Anne Ficklen
Editor: Adam Kowit
Editorial Assistant: Cecily McAndrews
Production Director: Diana Cisek
Manufacturing Manager: Tom Hyland
Design Director: Ken Carlson, Waterbury Publications, Inc.
Associate Design Director: Doug Samuelson, Waterbury Publications, Inc.
Senior Designer: Chad Jewell, Waterbury Publications, Inc.
Production Assistant: Mindy Samuelson, Waterbury Publications, Inc.

Our seal assures you that every recipe in *Dinner Express* has been
tested in the Better Homes and Gardens® Test Kitchen. This means
that each recipe is practical and reliable and meets our high standards
of taste appeal. We guarantee your satisfaction with this book for as
long as you own it.

From squeezing in tasty meals on hectic weeknights to feeding spur-of-the-moment guests, you face lots of cooking challenges. *Dinner Express* will help you handle them all.

It's loaded with nearly 200 family-pleasing recipes—each one perfected in the Better Homes and Gardens® Test Kitchen to work without a hitch.

Because main dishes are the focus of any meal, you'll find dozens of ways to get yourself out of that what-should-I-fix jam. As a bonus, we've included a chapter of supereasy main dishes that each use only five ingredients. What's more, when you decide it's time for a party, rely on our company-special entrées. They're so delicious, your guests will think you spent hours in the kitchen.

When you're looking for something to round out a meal, tap into the sensational side-dish ideas. And, if you're tempted to settle for store-bought snacks and desserts, our great-tasting options will convince you there's nothing like homemade, especially when the recipe takes just minutes.

With the choices in *Dinner Express,* you'll be amazed at how easy preparing satisfying meals can be—no matter what the occasion or how tight your schedule.

—Lynn Blanchard
Better Homes and Gardens®
Test Kitchen Director

Quick Honey-Garlic Pot Roast

weekday
main dishes

Preparing dinner day in and day out just got easier with this creative collection of everyday entrées. All your family's favorite foods are here—pot roast, burgers, stews, casseroles, and more. Each recipe has been streamlined to minimize kitchen time.

Quick Honey-Garlic Pot Roast

Imagine a comforting pot roast dinner in only 30 minutes. Thanks to precooked meat, all you have to do is add a few ingredients to give it a personal touch.

Prep: 10 minutes   **Cook:** 20 minutes
Makes 4 servings

1	17-ounce package refrigerated cooked beef roast au jus or beef pot roast with juices
2	tablespoons honey
1	tablespoon Worcestershire sauce
1	to 1½ teaspoons bottled roasted minced garlic
¼	teaspoon ground black pepper
2	cups packaged peeled baby carrots
12	ounces small red potatoes, quartered
1	medium red onion, cut into thin wedges Snipped fresh parsley (optional)

1. Remove meat from package, reserving juices. In a medium bowl, combine reserved juices, honey, Worcestershire sauce, roasted garlic, and pepper. Place meat in a large nonstick skillet. Arrange carrots, potatoes, and onion wedges around meat. Pour honey mixture over meat and vegetables.

2. Bring mixture to boiling; reduce heat. Cover and simmer for 20 to 25 minutes or until vegetables are tender and meat is heated through. Transfer meat and vegetables to a serving platter. Spoon sauce over meat and vegetables. If desired, sprinkle with snipped parsley.

Per serving: 305 cal., 9 g total fat (4 g sat. fat), 64 mg chol., 502 mg sodium, 35 g carb., 4 g fiber, 26 g pro.

Beef Ragout

There is nothing more comforting on a cold day than a steaming hot, thick, and savory beef stew. The cheddar cheese soup and the sour cream add a rich creaminess.

Start to finish: 25 minutes
Makes 6 servings

10	ounces dried wide egg noodles
1	17-ounce package refrigerated cooked beef tips with gravy
1	10.75-ounce can condensed cheddar cheese soup
1	9-ounce package frozen Italian-style green beans
1	4.5-ounce jar (drained weight) whole mushrooms, drained
½	cup water
3	tablespoons tomato paste
2	tablespoons dried minced onion
½	cup dairy sour cream

1. Prepare noodles according to package directions. Drain and keep warm.

2. Meanwhile, in a 4-quart Dutch oven, combine beef tips with gravy, soup, green beans, mushrooms, the water, tomato paste, and dried minced onion. Bring to boiling; reduce heat. Simmer, covered, for 10 to 15 minutes or until green beans are crisp-tender, stirring occasionally. Stir in sour cream; cook for 2 to 3 minutes more or until heated through. Serve over hot cooked noodles.

Per serving: 378 cal., 13 g total fat (5 g sat. fat), 90 mg chol., 954 mg sodium, 49 g carbo., 4 g fiber, 22 g pro.

Skillet Pot Roast with Mushrooms and Cherries

This boldly seasoned pot roast is ready to serve in only 30 minutes, just right for a weeknight meal.

Start to finish: 30 minutes
Makes 4 to 6 servings

1	12-ounce package frozen unsweetened pitted dark sweet cherries
8	ounces fresh button mushrooms, halved (3 cups)
1	medium red sweet pepper, cut into bite-size strips (¾ cup)
1	large onion, chopped (1 cup)
2	tablespoons snipped fresh herb, such as sage or thyme, or 2 teaspoons dried sage or thyme, crushed
1	tablespoon olive oil or cooking oil
2	16- to 17-ounce package refrigerated cooked beef pot roast with juices
2	tablespoons balsamic vinegar

1. Place frozen cherries in colander. Run cold water over cherries to partially thaw. Set aside; drain well.

2. In a 12-inch skillet, cook mushrooms, sweet pepper, onion, and 1 tablespoon of the herb in hot oil about 7 minutes or until tender.

3. Add pot roasts and juices, cherries, and balsamic vinegar to skillet. Bring to boiling; reduce heat. Simmer, uncovered, for 10 minutes or until heated through and juices thicken slightly, stirring occasionally. Sprinkle with remaining herb; stir to combine.

Per serving: 420 cal., 17 g total fat (5 g sat. fat), 104 mg chol., 1,174 mg sodium, 31 g carbo., 3 g fiber, 40 g pro.

Skillet Pot Roast with Mushrooms and Cherries

Sweet Potato–Roast Beef Hash

An appealing blend of sweet and regular potatoes makes this hash a cut above the ordinary.

Start to finish: 30 minutes
Makes 4 servings

- 1 medium sweet potato, peeled and diced
- 3 medium potatoes, peeled and diced
- ½ cup chopped onion
- ⅓ cup chopped red sweet pepper
- 2 tablespoons cooking oil
- 8 ounces cooked roast beef, cubed
- 4 eggs
- 2 green onions, chopped
  Salt
  Ground black pepper

1. In a covered large saucepan, cook diced potatoes in a small amount of boiling water for 3 minutes. Drain; cool slightly.

2. In a large nonstick skillet, cook onion and sweet pepper in hot oil until tender. Stir in cooked potatoes. Cook and stir about 5 minutes or just until tender. Stir in roast beef.

3. Using the back of a large spoon, make four depressions in the roast beef mixture. Break an egg into each depression. Cook, covered, over medium-low heat about 5 minutes or until the egg whites are completely set and yolks begin to thicken but are not hard. Sprinkle with green onion. Season to taste with salt and black pepper.

Per serving: 420 cal., 19 g total fat (5 g sat. fat), 257 mg chol., 154 mg sodium, 38 g carb., 4 g fiber, 25 g pro.

Italian Meatball Soup

What to do with the leftover packaged meatballs? Another night, pair them with prepared pasta sauce for a quick, classic spaghetti-and-meatball dinner.

Prep: 15 minutes **Cook:** 10 minutes
Makes 4 servings

- 1 14½-ounce can diced tomatoes with onion and garlic, undrained
- 1 14-ounce can beef broth
- 1½ cups water
- ½ teaspoon Italian seasoning, crushed
- ½ of a 16-ounce package frozen cooked meatballs
- ½ cup small dried pasta (such as elbow macaroni, orzo [rosamarina], tripolini, ditalini, or stellini)
- 1 cup loose-pack frozen mixed vegetables
  Shredded or shaved Parmesan cheese

1. In a large saucepan, stir together undrained tomatoes, beef broth, the water, and Italian seasoning; bring to boiling.

2. Add frozen meatballs, uncooked pasta, and frozen vegetables. Return to boiling; reduce heat. Cover and simmer about 10 minutes or until pasta and vegetables are tender. Top individual servings with Parmesan cheese.

Per serving: 337 cal., 16 g total fat (7 g sat. fat), 42 mg chol., 1,419 mg sodium, 31 g carb., 4 g fiber, 18 g pro.

With the ingredients on hand and the recipe for this **hearty soup** flagged and waiting, you'll always have something **filling and wonderful that can be ready in a hurry.**

Italian Meatball Soup

Penne with Meat Sauce

Penne with Meat Sauce

Quick-to-grab ingredients make this hearty pasta dish super easy.

Start to finish: 25 minutes
Makes 6 servings

8	ounces dried penne
1	pound lean ground beef
½	cup chopped onion
1	14-ounce can whole Italian-style tomatoes, undrained
½	of a 6-ounce can Italian-style tomato paste
¼	cup dry red wine or tomato juice
½	teaspoon sugar
½	teaspoon dried oregano, crushed
¼	teaspoon ground black pepper
¼	cup sliced pitted ripe olives
½	cup shredded reduced-fat mozzarella cheese (2 ounces)
	Fresh oregano leaves (optional)

1. Cook pasta according to package directions. Drain well. Return pasta to hot pan; cover to keep warm.

2. Meanwhile, in a very large skillet, cook ground beef and onion until beef is brown and onion is tender. Drain off fat. In a blender or food processor, combine undrained tomatoes, tomato paste, dry red wine, sugar, dried oregano, and pepper. Cover and blend or process until smooth.

3. Stir tomato mixture into beef mixture in skillet. Bring to boiling; reduce heat. Cover and simmer for 10 minutes. Stir in cooked pasta and olives. Cover and heat through.

4. Sprinkle individual servings with mozzarella cheese. If desired, garnish with oregano leaves.

Per serving: 339 cal., 11 g total fat (4 g sat. fat), 59 mg chol., 349 mg sodium, 33 g carb., 3 g fiber, 24 g pro.

Spaghetti with Cincinnati-Style Marinara

Cincinnati natives enjoy their chili over spaghetti. This versatile recipe lets you create the traditional Ohio favorite in almost no time.

Start to finish: 30 minutes
Makes 6 servings

12	ounces dried spaghetti
1	pound ground beef
1	cup chopped onion
1	to 2 tablespoons chili powder
¼	teaspoon ground cinnamon
1	15-ounce can red kidney beans, rinsed and drained
1	14-ounce jar marinara sauce
½	cup water
1	cup shredded cheddar cheese (4 ounces)

1. Cook spaghetti according to package directions. Meanwhile, in a large skillet, cook ground beef and onion until beef is brown and onion is tender. Drain off fat. Stir chili powder and cinnamon into beef mixture; cook and stir for 2 minutes.

2. Add kidney beans, marinara sauce, and the water. Cook over medium heat until mixture is boiling, stirring occasionally.

3. Place hot cooked spaghetti in a large serving bowl. Spoon beef mixture over spaghetti; sprinkle with cheddar cheese.

Per serving: 522 cal., 17 g total fat (7 g sat. fat), 67 mg chol., 527 mg sodium, 62 g carb., 7 g fiber, 32 g pro.

Five-Spice Steak Wraps

These wraps unite Asian and Mexican cuisine into one fresh, fused dish.

Start to finish: 25 minutes
Makes 4 servings

12	ounces boneless beef round steak
2	cups packaged shredded cabbage with carrot (coleslaw mix)
¼	cup thin strips red and/or green sweet pepper
¼	cup thin strips carrot
¼	cup snipped fresh chives
2	tablespoons rice vinegar
½	teaspoon toasted sesame oil
½	teaspoon five-spice powder
¼	teaspoon salt
	Nonstick cooking spray
¼	cup plain low-fat yogurt or light dairy sour cream
4	8-inch flour tortillas

1. If desired, partially freeze steak for easier slicing. Trim fat from steak. Thinly slice steak across the grain into bite-size strips; set aside.

2. In a medium bowl, combine coleslaw mix, sweet pepper, carrot, and chives. In a small bowl, combine rice vinegar and sesame oil. Pour vinegar mixture over coleslaw mixture; toss to coat. Set aside.

3. Sprinkle steak with five-spice powder and salt. Coat an unheated large nonstick skillet with nonstick cooking spray. Preheat over medium-high heat. Add steak strips; stir-fry for 3 to 4 minutes or until brown.

4. To assemble, spread *1 tablespoon* of the yogurt down the center of *each* tortilla. Top with steak strips. Stir coleslaw mixture; spoon over steak. Fold in sides of tortillas. If desired, secure with toothpicks or short skewers.

Per serving: 237 cal., 7 g total fat (2 g sat. fat), 51 mg chol., 329 mg sodium, 20 g carb., 2 g fiber, 22 g pro.

Reuben Quesadillas

Yum! All the flavors of the traditional corned beef sandwich are baked in these blankets of flour tortillas that turn crispy and golden.

Prep: 15 minutes **Bake:** 10 minutes
Oven: 375°F
Makes 4 servings

2   tablespoons cooking oil
½   of a medium sweet onion (such as Vidalia, Maui, or Walla Walla), halved and thinly sliced (about 1½ cups)
1   cup sauerkraut, drained
1   teaspoon caraway seeds
4   10-inch flour tortillas
¼   cup bottled Thousand Island salad dressing
8   ounces thinly sliced corned beef, cut into strips
1   cup shredded Swiss cheese (4 ounces)

1. Preheat oven to 375°F. In a medium skillet, heat 1 tablespoon of the oil over medium heat. Add onion; cook until tender. Add sauerkraut and ½ teaspoon of the caraway seeds; cook for 2 to 3 minutes or until any liquid is evaporated.

2. Brush some of the remaining 1 tablespoon oil over *two* of the tortillas. Place, oiled sides down, on two large pizza pans or baking sheets. Spread salad dressing over tortillas. Top with corned beef, onion mixture, and Swiss cheese. Top with remaining tortillas. Brush with remaining oil; sprinkle with the remaining ½ teaspoon caraway seeds. Bake about 10 minutes or until cheese is melted. Cut into wedges to serve.

Per serving: 514 cal., 34 g total fat (11 g sat. fat), 85 mg chol., 1,371 mg sodium, 29 g carb., 2 g fiber, 21 g pro.

Skillet Tostadas

If you can't find tostada shells, substitute taco shells, still plan on two per serving.

Start to finish: 25 minutes
Makes 4 servings

8   ounces ground beef
½   cup chopped onion
1   15-ounce can light red kidney beans, rinsed and drained
1   11-ounce can condensed nacho cheese soup
⅓   cup purchased salsa
8   tostada shells
1   cup shredded taco cheese (4 ounces)
    Shredded lettuce
    Chopped tomatoes
    Dairy sour cream and/or guacamole (optional)

1. In a 10-inch skillet, cook ground beef and onion until beef is brown and onion is tender. Drain off fat. Stir kidney beans, nacho cheese soup, and salsa into beef mixture. Heat through.

2. Divide beef-salsa mixture among tostada shells. Top with cheese. Top with lettuce and tomatoes. If desired, serve with sour cream and/or guacamole.

Per serving: 576 cal., 33 g total fat (15 g sat. fat), 81 mg chol., 1,277 mg sodium, 42 g carb., 11 g fiber, 26 g pro.

Serve-Yourself Tostadas

Don't take the time to assemble Skillet Tostadas individually. Set up a serving "bar" instead and let everyone build a custom tostada. Just leave the filling in the skillet, set out the cheese and toppers in separate bowls, and stack the tostada shells in a basket.

Individual Sicilian Meat Loaves

If you like, make these loaves with ground pork or bulk mild Italian sausage instead of ground beef. Or even better, how about mixing all three?

Prep: 10 minutes **Bake:** 20 minutes
Oven: 400°F
Makes 4 servings

- 1 egg, beaten
- 1 14-ounce jar garlic-and-onion tomato-based pasta sauce (1¾ cups)
- ¼ cup seasoned fine dry bread crumbs
- ¼ teaspoon salt
- ¼ teaspoon ground black pepper
- 12 ounces ground beef
- 2 ounces mozzarella cheese
- 4 thin slices prosciutto or cooked ham (about 2 ounces)
- 1 9-ounce package refrigerated plain or spinach fettuccine
  Finely shredded Parmesan cheese (optional)

1. Preheat oven to 400°F. In a medium bowl, combine egg, ¼ cup of the pasta sauce, the fine dry bread crumbs, salt, and pepper. Add ground beef; mix well.

2. Cut mozzarella cheese into four logs, each measuring about 2¼ × ¾ × ½ inches. Wrap one slice of the prosciutto or ham around *each* cheese log. Shape one-fourth of the ground beef mixture around *each* cheese log to form a loaf. Flatten each meat loaf to 1½ inches thick; place in a shallow baking pan.

3. Bake meat loaves about 20 minutes or until done (160°F).

4. Meanwhile, cook pasta according to package directions. In a small saucepan, heat remaining pasta sauce over medium heat until bubbly.

5. Arrange meat loaves over hot cooked pasta. Spoon sauce over top. If desired, sprinkle with Parmesan cheese.

Per serving: 631 cal., 31 g total fat (12 g sat. fat), 173 mg chol., 1,132 mg sodium, 55 g carb., 3 g fiber, 31 g pro.

Easy Shepherd's Pie

To quick-thaw the frozen mixed vegetables, place them in a colander and rinse with running water for a minute.

Start to finish: 30 minutes
Makes 6 servings

- 1 pound ground beef or uncooked ground turkey or chicken
- ½ cup chopped onion
- 1 10-ounce package frozen mixed vegetables, thawed
- ¼ cup water
- 1 10¾-ounce can condensed tomato soup
- 1 teaspoon Worcestershire sauce
- ¼ teaspoon dried thyme, crushed
- 1 20-ounce package refrigerated mashed potatoes or 3 cups leftover mashed potatoes
- ½ cup shredded cheddar cheese (2 ounces)

1. In a large skillet, cook ground meat and onion until meat is brown and onion is tender. Drain off fat. Stir vegetables and the water into meat mixture. Bring to boiling; reduce heat. Cover; simmer about 5 minutes or until vegetables are tender.

2. Stir in tomato soup, Worcestershire sauce, and thyme. Return to boiling; reduce heat. Drop mashed potatoes in six mounds on top of the hot mixture. Sprinkle potatoes with shredded cheddar cheese. Cover and simmer for 10 to 15 minutes or until potatoes are heated through.

Per serving: 301 cal., 12 g total fat (5 g sat. fat), 58 mg chol., 570 mg sodium, 27 g carb., 3 g fiber, 20 g pro.

Think there's no time to bake meat loaf tonight? Think again. **Mini loaves cut the cooking time remarkably.** Speaking of remarkable, you'll love the **oozy mozzarella filling.**

Individual Sicilian Meat Loaves

Bail-Out Beef Stroganoff

The horseradish–sour cream topper
and broccoli add **extra flavor** to this
fast-fix version of an **old-world classic.**

Bail-Out Beef Stroganoff

To save the time and work it takes to cut up broccoli, stop by your supermarket's salad bar and pick up precut florets.

Start to finish: 30 minutes
Makes 4 servings

3	cups dried wide noodles
3	cups broccoli florets (12 ounces)
½	cup light dairy sour cream
1½	teaspoons prepared horseradish
½	teaspoon fresh dill
1	pound beef ribeye steak
1	small onion, cut into ½-inch-thick slices
½	teaspoon bottled minced garlic
1	tablespoon cooking oil
4	teaspoons all-purpose flour
½	teaspoon ground black pepper
1	14-ounce can beef broth
3	tablespoons tomato paste
1	teaspoon Worcestershire sauce

1. Cook noodles according to package directions, adding broccoli for the last 5 minutes of cooking. Drain well. Return pasta mixture to hot pan; cover to keep warm.

2. Meanwhile, in a small serving bowl, stir together the sour cream, horseradish, and dill; cover and chill until serving time.

3. Trim fat from beef. Cut beef into bite-size strips. In a large skillet, cook and stir half of the beef, the onion, and garlic in hot oil until onion is tender and beef is desired doneness. Remove from skillet. Add remaining beef to skillet; cook and stir until beef is desired doneness. Return all of the beef to the skillet; sprinkle flour and pepper over beef. Stir to coat.

4. Stir in broth, tomato paste, and Worcestershire sauce. Cook and stir until thickened and bubbly. Cook and stir for 1 minute more. Divide noodle-broccoli mixture among four individual bowls. Spoon the beef mixture on top of the noodle mixture. Top with the horseradish–sour cream mixture.

Per serving: 413 cal., 16 g total fat (6 g sat. fat), 103 mg chol., 504 mg sodium, 33 g carb., 3 g fiber, 33 g pro.

Beef Bunburgers

These could be called "family burgers" because they're a great choice for a kid-friendly meal. Team them with chips, dip, and a deli salad and you'll have a sure-to-please supper.

Prep: 15 minutes   **Cook:** 15 minutes
Makes 8 servings

1½	pounds ground beef
½	cup chopped onion
⅓	cup chopped green sweet pepper
1	10¾-ounce can condensed tomato soup
1	tablespoon vinegar
1	teaspoon dry mustard
1	teaspoon poultry seasoning
½	teaspoon dried thyme, crushed
¼	teaspoon salt
8	hamburger buns, split and toasted

1. In a large skillet, cook ground beef, onion, and sweet pepper until beef is brown and onion is tender. Drain well. Stir tomato soup, vinegar, dry mustard, poultry seasoning, thyme, and salt into beef mixture in skillet.

2. Bring to boiling; reduce heat. Simmer, uncovered, about 15 minutes or until desired consistency. Serve on toasted hamburger buns.

Per serving: 364 cal., 19 g total fat (7 g sat. fat), 62 mg chol., 584 mg sodium, 28 g carb., 2 g fiber, 20 g pro.

These are no ordinary burgers—the moist, juicy patties are flavored with a zesty brush-on of ketchup, Worcestershire sauce, and steak sauce then **topped with fiery salsa.**

All-American Burgers

All-American Burgers

If you love cheeseburgers, add a slice of cheddar, Swiss, or pepper cheese to this favorite.

Prep: 10 minutes   **Grill:** 14 minutes
Makes 4 servings

- 2 **tablespoons ketchup**
- 1 **tablespoon Worcestershire sauce**
- 1 **tablespoon bottled steak sauce**
- 1 **teaspoon sugar**
- 1 **teaspoon cooking oil**
- 1 **teaspoon vinegar**
- ½ **teaspoon bottled minced garlic**
  or 2 tablespoons finely chopped onion
  Few dashes bottled hot pepper sauce
- 1 **pound lean ground beef**
- ¼ **teaspoon salt**
- ¼ **teaspoon ground black pepper**
- 4 **whole wheat hamburger buns, split and toasted**
  Fresh 'n' Spicy Salsa
  Lettuce, cornichons, radish halves, and/or cucumber slices (optional)

1. For sauce: In a small saucepan, combine ketchup, Worcestershire sauce, steak sauce, sugar, oil, vinegar, garlic or onion, and hot pepper sauce. Bring to boiling; reduce heat. Simmer, uncovered, for 5 minutes. Set aside.

2. In a medium bowl, combine ground beef, salt, and black pepper; mix well. Shape meat mixture into four ¾-inch-thick patties.

3. Place patties on the rack of an uncovered grill directly over medium coals. Grill for 14 to 18 minutes or until done (160°F),* turning once and brushing often with sauce. Discard any remaining sauce.

4. Serve burgers on buns topped with Fresh 'n' Spicy Salsa. If desired, serve with lettuce, cornichons, radish halves, and/or cucumber slices.

Fresh 'n' Spicy Salsa: In a medium bowl, stir together 1 cup seeded and chopped yellow and/or red tomatoes; 3 tablespoons finely chopped red onion; 1 to 2 tablespoons snipped fresh cilantro; 1 fresh serrano chile pepper, finely chopped (seeded, if desired) (see tip, page 58); 1 tablespoon lime juice; and, if desired, 1 teaspoon honey. Cover and chill until serving time. Makes about 1 cup.

Per serving: 336 cal., 15 g total fat (5 g sat. fat), 71 mg chol., 572 mg sodium, 26 g carb., 2 g fiber, 25 g pro.

*Test Kitchen Tip: The internal color of a burger is not a reliable doneness indicator. A beef patty cooked to 160°F is safe, regardless of color. To measure the doneness of a patty, insert an instant-read thermometer through the side of the patty to a depth of 2 to 3 inches.

Ready, Set, Grill

When it comes to grilling, a few pointers can help you make the most of your time and grill.

• Igniting your gas grill or lighting coals for the charcoal grill should be done first whenever you're preparing a grilled recipe. Using a chimney starter helps make sure the coals light quickly and easily.

• To check the temperature of coals, carefully place the palm of your hand just above the grill rack and count the number of seconds you can hold it in that position. Two seconds indicates a hot fire, four seconds a medium fire, and six seconds a low fire.

• Fat and meat juices dripping onto hot coals may cause flare-ups. To control them, raise the grill rack, cover the grill, space the hot coals farther apart, or remove a few coals. As a last resort, remove the food from the grill and mist the fire with water from a spray bottle. To prevent flare-ups on a gas grill, after each use turn the grill setting to high for 10 to 15 minutes with the lid closed. Then use a brass-bristle brush to remove any baked-on food from the grill rack. Reheating the grill also will help burn off residue on lava rock or ceramic briquettes.

Creamy Ranch Chicken

Kids will love this dish of creamed chicken over noodles with the **tanginess of ranch dressing.** Round out the meal with a tossed salad and **crusty bread.**

Creamy Ranch Chicken

Start to finish: 30 minutes
Makes 4 servings

6   slices bacon
4   skinless, boneless chicken breast halves,
      cut into bite-size pieces
2   tablespoons all-purpose flour
2   tablespoons ranch dry salad dressing mix
1¼ cups milk
3   cups dried medium noodles
1   tablespoon finely shredded Parmesan
      cheese

1. Cut bacon into narrow strips. In a large skillet, cook bacon over medium heat until crisp. Drain bacon on paper towels; discard all but 2 tablespoons drippings.

2. In the same skillet, cook chicken in reserved drippings until tender and no longer pink, turning to brown evenly. Sprinkle flour and salad dressing mix over the chicken in the skillet; stir well. Stir in milk. Cook and stir until thickened and bubbly. Cook and stir 1 minute more. Stir in bacon.

3. Meanwhile, cook noodles according to package directions. Serve chicken mixture with noodles; sprinkle with Parmesan.

Per serving: 488 cal., 18 g total fat (7 g sat. fat), 137 mg chol., 574 mg sodium, 27 g carbo., 1 g fiber, 45 g pro.

Triple-Mango Chicken

Mango chutney, fruit, and juice add a refreshing, exotic accent to this chicken dish. When choosing a fresh mango, gently press against the fruit with your thumb. It should give slightly. The stem end should smell fresh and sweet.

Start to finish: 20 minutes
Makes 4 servings

4   small skinless, boneless chicken breast
      halves
1   tablespoon olive oil
1   mango, seeded, peeled, and cubed
½   cup mango-blend fruit drink*
¼   cup mango chutney
2   medium zucchini, thinly sliced lengthwise
    Salt
    Crushed red pepper

1. In very large skillet, cook chicken in hot oil over medium heat for 6 minutes; turn chicken. Add mango cubes, mango drink, and chutney. Cook for 4 to 6 minutes or until chicken is no longer pink, stirring occasionally.

2. Meanwhile, place zucchini and 14 cup water in a microwave-safe 2-quart square dish. Cover with vented plastic wrap. Microwave on 100% power (high) for 2 to 3 minutes, stirring once; drain. Serve chicken with zucchini. Season with salt and crushed red pepper.

Per serving: 274 cal., 9 g total fat (1 g sat. fat), 66 mg chol., 277 mg sodium, 22 g carbo., 2 g fiber, 28 g pro.

*Test Kitchen Tip: Mango nectar, carrot juice, or orange juice may be substituted for the mango-blend drink.

Chicken and Pasta in Peanut Sauce

The safest way to cut the chicken breasts in half horizontally is to lay a breast flat on the work surface. Place one hand firmly on top of the chicken, pressing down lightly to hold it steady. Use the other hand to hold the knife horizontally and cut through the meat.

Start to finish: 20 minutes
Makes 4 servings

8   ounces dried thin spaghetti
1   bunch broccolini, cut into 2-inch lengths
1   medium red sweet pepper, cut into
       bite-size strips
1   pound skinless, boneless chicken
       breast halves
    Salt and ground black pepper
1   tablespoon olive oil
½   cup bottled peanut sauce
    Crushed red pepper (optional)

1. In a Dutch oven, cook spaghetti following package directions, adding broccolini and sweet pepper during the last 2 minutes of cooking. Drain. Return pasta and vegetables to Dutch oven; set aside.

2. Meanwhile, halve chicken breasts horizontally. Sprinkle chicken with salt and pepper. In an extra-large skillet, heat olive oil over medium-high heat. Add chicken; cook about 4 minutes or until chicken is no longer pink (170°F), turning once halfway through cooking. Transfer chicken to a cutting board. Slice chicken; add to pasta and vegetables. Heat through. Add peanut sauce. Pass crushed red pepper.

Per serving: 467 cal., 10 g total fat (2 g sat. fat), 66 mg chol., 634 mg sodium, 55 g carb., 5 g dietary fiber, 37 g protein.

Fettuccine with Cherry Tomatoes

Start to finish: 20 minutes
Makes 4 servings

1   9-ounce package refrigerated fettuccine,
       cut into thirds
½   cup shredded Parmesan cheese
2   tablespoons olive oil
1   6- to 9-ounce package refrigerated or
       frozen Italian-flavor or grilled-cooked
       chicken breast strips, thawed if frozen
1   pint cherry tomatoes, halved
½   cup pitted ripe olives, halved
    Salt and freshly ground black pepper

1. In a Dutch oven, cook pasta according to package directions. Drain and return to pan.

2. Add cheese, oil, and chicken. Return to low heat; toss to coat and heat through. Remove from heat. Add tomatoes and olives. Season with salt and pepper to taste and toss again. Serve immediately.

Per serving: 371 cal., 15 g total fat (4 g sat. fat), 76 mg chol., 866 mg sodium, 39 g carbo., 3 g fiber, 22 g pro.

This quick-to-fix pasta toss **is perfect for** the dog days of summer. **Fresh-from-the-vine cherry tomatoes** are guaranteed to energize your taste buds.

Fettuccine with Cherry Tomatoes

Szechwan-Fried Chicken Breasts

Szechwan-Fried Chicken Breasts

Szechwan Chinese cuisine is known for its hot, spicy dishes. The chile oil spikes up the heat, but the sweetness from the apricot preserves tempers it.

Start to finish: 30 minutes
Makes 4 servings

1	tablespoon soy sauce
1	teaspoon grated fresh ginger
1	teaspoon chile oil
½	teaspoon sugar
½	cup all-purpose flour
4	skinless, boneless chicken breast halves (1¼ to 1½ pounds total)
1	tablespoon cooking oil
¼	cup apricot preserves
¼	cup chicken broth
	Shredded orange peel (optional)
	Snipped fresh chives (optional)
	Hot cooked rice (optional)

1. In a small bowl, stir together soy sauce, ginger, ½ teaspoon of the chile oil, and the sugar; set aside.

2. Place flour in a shallow bowl. Brush both sides of each chicken breast half with soy sauce mixture; dip in flour to coat. In a large nonstick skillet, heat cooking oil over medium-high heat. Add chicken; cook for 8 to 10 minutes or until tender and no longer pink (170°F), turning once. Remove chicken from skillet; cover and keep warm.

3. For sauce: Add apricot preserves, chicken broth, and the remaining ½ teaspoon chile oil to skillet. Cook and stir over medium heat until preserves melt and mixture is heated through. Spoon sauce over chicken. If desired, sprinkle with orange peel. If desired, stir chives into hot cooked rice; serve with the chicken.

Per serving: 315 cal., 7 g total fat (1 g sat. fat), 82 mg chol., 374 mg sodium, 25 g carb., 1 g fiber, 35 g pro.

Southwestern Chicken Wraps

These Tex-Mex–influenced sandwich rolls are perfect for a meal on a sweltering summer day. Because they use precooked chicken strips, no cooking is necessary.

Start to finish: 15 minutes
Makes 4 servings

½	cup dairy sour cream
2	tablespoons purchased guacamole
4	10-inch dried tomato, spinach, and/or plain flour tortillas
2	5½-ounce packages Southwestern-flavored refrigerated cooked chicken breast strips
2	plum tomatoes, sliced
2	cups shredded lettuce

1. In a small bowl, stir together sour cream and guacamole. Divide sour cream mixture among tortillas, spreading over one side of each tortilla. Divide chicken, tomatoes, and lettuce among tortillas. Roll up.

Per serving: 395 cal., 13 g total fat (4 g sat. fat), 49 mg chol., 1,015 mg sodium, 45 g carb., 2 g fiber, 25 g pro.

Testing Doneness

An instant-read thermometer is invaluable for testing the doneness of foods. To use one, insert the tip into the center of the food, making sure it does not touch bone and that it is at least ½ inch into the food. Wait 10 to 15 seconds for the temperature to stabilize. If the food is not at the recommended temperature, cook it a little longer and recheck it in a different spot.

Barbecued Chicken Thighs

Serve this lip-smacking-good chicken with coleslaw and baked beans from the deli section of your supermarket.

Prep: 10 minutes   **Grill:** 12 minutes
Makes 4 servings

¼   cup packed brown sugar
2   tablespoons finely chopped onion
2   tablespoons vinegar
1   tablespoon yellow mustard
¼   teaspoon celery seeds
⅛   teaspoon garlic powder
1   teaspoon paprika
¼   teaspoon salt
¼   teaspoon ground black pepper
8   skinless, boneless chicken thighs

1. For sauce: In a small saucepan, combine brown sugar, onion, vinegar, mustard, celery seeds, and garlic powder. Bring to boiling, stirring until sugar dissolves. Set aside.

2. In a small bowl, combine paprika, salt, and pepper. Sprinkle paprika mixture evenly over chicken thighs; rub in with your fingers.

3. Place chicken thighs on the rack of an uncovered grill over medium coals. Grill for 12 to 15 minutes or until no longer pink (180°F), turning once halfway through grilling and brushing with sauce during the last 5 minutes of grilling.

Per serving: 305 cal., 8 g total fat (2 g sat. fat), 158 mg chol., 329 mg sodium, 16 g carb., 0 g fiber, 40 g pro.

Broiling Directions: Preheat broiler. Place chicken thighs on the unheated rack of a broiler pan. Broil 4 to 5 inches from heat for 12 to 15 minutes or until no longer pink (180°F), turning once halfway through broiling and brushing with sauce during the last 5 minutes of broiling.

Sweet-and-Sour Chicken

Sweet-and-sour chicken is a favorite of all ages. With this streamlined recipe, you can make it quickly—without deep frying!

Start to finish: 25 minutes
Makes 4 or 5 servings

1   8-ounce can pineapple chunks (juice pack)
½   cup bottled sweet-and-sour sauce
12   ounces skinless, boneless chicken breast halves, cut into 1-inch pieces
1   tablespoon reduced-sodium soy sauce
4   teaspoons cooking oil
1   medium red sweet pepper, cut into bite-size strips
1   medium carrot, sliced
1   cup fresh pea pods, stems removed
2   cups hot cooked rice

1. Drain pineapple, reserving 2 tablespoons of the juice; set pineapple chunks aside. In a small bowl, stir together the reserved pineapple juice and the sweet-and-sour sauce; set aside. In a medium bowl, toss chicken with soy sauce; set aside.

2. In a large nonstick skillet, heat 3 teaspoons of the oil over medium-high heat. Add sweet pepper and carrot; cook for 3 minutes. Add pea pods; cook and stir about 1 minute more or until vegetables are crisp-tender. Remove from skillet; set aside.

3. Add the remaining 1 teaspoon oil to skillet. Using a slotted spoon, add chicken to skillet. Cook and stir for 3 to 4 minutes or until chicken is no longer pink. Add sweet-and-sour sauce mixture, vegetable mixture, and pineapple chunks; heat through. Serve chicken mixture with hot cooked rice.

Per serving: 337 cal., 6 g total fat (1 g sat. fat), 49 mg chol., 297 mg sodium, 46 g carb., 3 g fiber, 23 g pro.

Sweet-and-Sour Chicken

Spring Chicken Scaloppine

For this poultry version of scaloppine, thinly pounded **chicken breasts are cooked quickly** in butter and topped with an **aromatic herb-and-wine sauce.**

Spring Chicken Scaloppine

For incredibly fresh flavor, use a combination of fresh herbs such as oregano, thyme, and/or mint.

Start to finish: 25 minutes
Makes 4 servings

4   skinless, boneless chicken breast halves
   (1¼ to 1½ pounds total)
¼   cup all-purpose flour
   Salt
4   tablespoons butter
½   cup dry white wine and/or chicken broth
¼   cup sliced green onions
½   cup snipped mixed fresh herbs
¼   teaspoon coarsely ground black pepper
   Steamed fresh asparagus* (optional)

1. Place each chicken piece between two pieces of plastic wrap. Working from the center to the edges, pound lightly with the flat side of a meat mallet until pieces are an even ¼-inch thickness. Remove plastic wrap. In shallow dish, combine flour and ¼ teaspoon salt. Coat chicken pieces with flour mixture.

2. In a 12-inch skillet, heat 2 tablespoons of the butter over medium heat. Add chicken; cook for 6 to 8 minutes or until chicken is tender and no longer pink, turning once. Transfer chicken to a serving platter; cover and keep warm.

3. Add wine and green onions to the skillet. Cook and stir for 1 minute, scraping up any browned bits from bottom of skillet. Cook about 1 minute more or until wine mixture is reduced to ⅓ cup. Remove from heat. Whisk in the remaining 2 tablespoons butter until melted. Stir in half of the snipped herbs, the pepper, and ⅛ teaspoon salt.** Drizzle wine sauce over individual servings; sprinkle with remaining herbs. If desired, serve with steamed asparagus.

Per serving: 317 cal., 14 g total fat (8 g sat. fat), 113 mg chol., 380 mg sodium, 7 g carb., 0 g fiber, 34 g pro.

*Test Kitchen Tip: To steam fresh asparagus, snap off and discard woody bases from the asparagus spears. Bias-slice asparagus into 1-inch-long pieces. Steam asparagus for 3 to 5 minutes or until tender.

**Test Kitchen Tip: If using chicken broth rather than wine, omit the ⅛ teaspoon salt.

Hungarian-Style Chicken

Hungarian cooks use paprika to add full flavor to dishes such as this one.

Start to finish: 30 minutes
Makes 6 servings

6   skinless, boneless chicken breast halves
   (about 2 pounds total)
2   teaspoons Hungarian paprika
3   tablespoons cooking oil
1   cup chopped onion
1   10¾-ounce can condensed cream of
   chicken soup
1   8-ounce carton dairy sour cream
¼   cup milk
   Hot cooked noodles

1. Sprinkle chicken with 1 teaspoon of the paprika. In a large skillet, heat 2 tablespoons of the oil over medium heat. Add chicken; cook for 8 to 10 minutes or until chicken is tender and no longer pink (170°F), turning once. Remove chicken from skillet; cover and keep warm.

2. In the same skillet, heat remaining 1 tablespoon oil over medium heat. Add onion; cook for 5 to 6 minutes or until tender.

3. Meanwhile, in a small bowl, combine cream of chicken soup, sour cream, milk, and the remaining 1 teaspoon paprika. Add to cooked onion; cook and stir until heated though. Serve sour cream mixture over chicken. Serve with hot cooked noodles.

Per serving: 485 cal., 22 g total fat (8 g sat. fat), 136 mg chol., 487 mg sodium, 29 g carb., 2 g fiber, 42 g pro.

Just a **pinch of saffron** goes a long way in **adding flavor and more intense color** to this elegant chicken and pasta soup. Spinach provides a **captivating contrast** to the saffron.

Tortellini Chicken Soup

Tortellini Chicken Soup

If the herb chicken tortellini isn't available at your supermarket, choose vegetable ravioli instead.

Start to finish: 25 minutes
Makes 4 servings

	Nonstick cooking spray
12	ounces skinless, boneless chicken breast halves, cut into ½-inch cubes
6	cups reduced-sodium chicken broth
½	cup sliced leek or chopped onion
1	tablespoon grated fresh ginger
¼	teaspoon saffron threads, slightly crushed (optional)
1	9-ounce package refrigerated herb chicken tortellini or vegetable ravioli
½	cup fresh baby spinach leaves or shredded fresh spinach

1. Lightly coat an unheated large saucepan with nonstick cooking spray. Preheat over medium-high heat. Add chicken; cook and stir for 3 minutes. Carefully add broth, leek or onion, ginger, and, if desired, saffron.

2. Bring to boiling. Add pasta. Return to boiling; reduce heat. Simmer, uncovered, for 5 to 9 minutes or until pasta is tender, stirring occasionally. Remove from heat. Top individual servings with spinach.

Per serving: 222 cal., 3 g total fat (0 g sat. fat), 59 mg chol., 1,221 mg sodium, 21 g carb., 3 g fiber, 29 g pro.

Golden-Crusted Chicken Pies

This no-fuss version of chicken pie is a little different—it combines minestrone soup and cream cheese in a delightful tomato-cream sauce.

Prep: 15 minutes   **Bake:** 12 minutes
Oven: 375°F
Makes 4 servings

¾	cup milk
4	teaspoons all-purpose flour
¼	teaspoon ground black pepper
1	10¾-ounce can condensed minestrone soup
2	cups cubed cooked chicken or turkey (about 10 ounces)
1	3-ounce package cream cheese, cubed
1	4.5-ounce package (5 or 6) refrigerated buttermilk or country-style biscuits

1. Preheat oven to 375°F. In a screw-top jar, combine milk, flour, and pepper. Cover and shake well. In a medium saucepan, stir milk mixture into minestrone soup. Cook and stir over medium heat until thickened and bubbly. Stir in chicken and cream cheese. Heat through, stirring to melt cream cheese.

2. Pour hot chicken mixture into four 10-ounce custard cups. Separate the biscuits; cut biscuits into quarters. Arrange five or six biscuit quarters on top of each custard cup.

3. Bake for 12 to 15 minutes or until biscuits are golden brown.

Per serving: 415 cal., 20 g total fat (8 g sat. fat), 92 mg chol., 1,139 mg sodium, 31 g carb., 3 g fiber, 28 g pro.

Buffalo-Style Chicken Strips with Blue Cheese

Work-saving chicken breast tenders make this homemade adaptation of restaurant-style Buffalo wings easy on the cook.
Start to finish: 25 minutes
Makes 4 servings

⅓ cup all-purpose flour
¾ teaspoon salt
½ teaspoon ground black pepper
¼ cup milk
1 pound chicken breast tenderloins
½ cup olive oil or cooking oil
4 teaspoons butter or margarine, melted
2 teaspoons bottled hot pepper sauce
⅓ cup bottled blue cheese salad dressing

1. In a shallow dish, combine flour, salt, and pepper. Pour milk into another shallow dish. Dip chicken in milk; coat with flour mixture.

2. In a large skillet, heat oil over medium heat. Add half of the chicken; cook about 4 minutes or until no longer pink (170°F), turning once. Repeat with remaining chicken.

3. Meanwhile, stir together melted butter and hot pepper sauce. Drizzle butter mixture over chicken strips. Serve chicken strips with blue cheese salad dressing for dipping.

Per serving: 369 cal., 24 g total fat (6 g sat. fat), 81 mg chol., 784 mg sodium, 10 g carb., 0 g fiber, 29 g pro.

Ginger Noodle Bowl

If you like, substitute button mushrooms for the shiitakes. Many supermarkets sell button mushrooms already cleaned and sliced.
Start to finish: 25 minutes
Makes 3 servings

2 cups dried Chinese egg noodles or fine egg noodles (4 ounces)
¼ teaspoon ground ginger
⅓ cup bottled stir-fry sauce
2 teaspoons peanut oil or cooking oil
1 cup fresh sugar snap peas or pea pods, tips and stems removed and cut up
1 cup sliced fresh shiitake mushrooms
1 small red sweet pepper, cut into bite-size strips
5 ounces cooked chicken breast, cut into strips (about 1 cup)
2 tablespoons cashews, broken

1. Cook noodles according to package directions. Drain; set aside. Stir ginger into the bottled stir-fry sauce; set aside.

2. In a large skillet, heat oil over medium-high heat. Add sugar snap peas, mushrooms, and sweet pepper; cook and stir for 3 to 5 minutes or until crisp-tender. Stir in cooked noodles, chicken, cashews, and stir-fry sauce mixture; heat through.

Per serving: 362 cal., 10 g total fat (2 g sat. fat), 77 mg chol., 734 mg sodium, 42 g carb., 4 g fiber, 25 g pro.

Ginger Noodle Bowl

Thanks to **bottled stir-fry sauce,** you can **whip up** this chicken, sugar snap pea, mushroom, and sweet pepper stir-fry on a **busy weeknight.**

Chicken in Phyllo Nests

Chicken in Phyllo Nests

Leftover grilled steak or chunks of cooked salmon are appetizing options for the chicken.

Start to finish: 25 minutes
Oven: 425°F
Makes 6 servings

	Nonstick cooking spray
10	sheets frozen phyllo dough (14×9-inch rectangles), thawed
2	tablespoons olive oil
1	cup 2-inch-long pieces green onions
12	ounces refrigerated grilled chicken breast strips, cut up (3 cups)
1	6-ounce package fresh baby spinach
¾	cup cherry tomatoes, halved or quartered (optional)
1	tablespoon snipped fresh tarragon
¼	teaspoon freshly ground black pepper
½	cup bottled balsamic vinaigrette salad dressing

1. Preheat oven to 425°F. Lightly coat a 15×10×1-inch baking pan with nonstick cooking spray; set aside. Roll stack of phyllo sheets into a cylinder shape. Using a sharp knife, cut phyllo crosswise into ¼- to ½-inch-wide slices. Gently separate phyllo into strips; spread strips evenly in the prepared baking pan. Coat phyllo generously with nonstick cooking spray. Bake 8 to 10 minutes or until phyllo is golden.

2. Meanwhile, in a 12-inch skillet, heat oil over medium-high heat. Add green onions; cook about 1 minute or just until tender. Add chicken; cook and stir until heated through. Remove skillet from heat. Add spinach, cherry tomatoes (if desired), tarragon, and pepper. Toss to combine.

3. Divide phyllo among six bowls. Spoon chicken mixture over phyllo. Drizzle with balsamic vinaigrette. Serve immediately.

Per serving: 197 cal., 10 g total fat (2 g sat. fat), 40 mg chol., 760 mg sodium, 14 g carb., 1 g fiber, 14 g pro.

Grilled Chicken and Kiwi Tacos

Fried flour tortillas give these terrific tacos a homemade flair. Another time, save a few minutes—and some mess—by using heated purchased taco shells.

Start to finish: 30 minutes
Makes 6 tacos

½	teaspoon ground cumin
¼	teaspoon salt
⅛	to ¼ teaspoon crushed red pepper
8	ounces skinless, boneless chicken breast halves
1	teaspoon cooking oil
	Fried Taco Shells
1	cup shredded romaine
½	cup shredded Monterey Jack cheese
3	kiwifruits, peeled and chopped
1	small tomato, chopped
1	tablespoon lime juice or lemon juice

1. In a small bowl, combine cumin, salt, and crushed red pepper. Brush chicken breasts with oil; sprinkle evenly with cumin mixture. Place each breast half between two pieces of plastic wrap; gently pound with flat side of a meat mallet to ½-inch thickness. Place chicken on the lightly oiled rack of an uncovered grill directly over medium-high coals. Grill for 6 to 8 minutes or until done (170°F), turning once. Remove chicken; set aside until cool enough to handle. Meanwhile, prepare Fried Taco Shells.

2. Cut chicken into strips; place in taco shells. Top with romaine and cheese. In a small bowl, combine kiwifruit, tomato, and lime juice. Sprinkle onto tacos.

Fried Taco Shells: In a heavy large skillet, heat ½ inch cooking oil over medium heat. Using six 5-inch flour tortillas, add tortillas, one at a time, to hot oil; cook just until golden. Using tongs, remove from hot oil. Fold fried tortillas over a paper-towel-wrapped rolling pin. Let cool until firm.

Per taco: 170 cal., 7 g total fat (3 g sat. fat), 30 mg chol., 219 mg sodium, 13 g carb., 2 g fiber, 13 g pro.

Chicken and Pasta

Bottled garlic, ginger, and pesto are a hurried cook's friends. You'll find them in your supermarket's produce section.

Start to finish: 30 minutes
Makes 4 servings

1½ **teaspoons coarsely ground pepper blend**
¾ **teaspoon salt**
½ **teaspoon bottled minced garlic**
4 **skinless, boneless chicken breasts (about 1¼ pounds total)**
2 **tablespoons olive oil**
2 **large onions, sliced**
3 **medium tomatoes, chopped**
1 **tablespoon tomato paste**
2 **to 3 teaspoons grated fresh ginger**
8 **ounces dried spaghetti**
¼ **cup purchased pesto**
   Parmesan cheese shards (optional)

1. In a small bowl, combine 1 teaspoon of the pepper blend, ½ teaspoon of the salt, and the garlic. Sprinkle evenly over chicken. In a large skillet, heat oil over medium heat. Add chicken and onions; cook about 15 minutes or until chicken is tender and no longer pink (170°F) and onions are tender, turning chicken once and stirring onions occasionally.

2. Remove chicken from skillet; slice crosswise into strips. Return chicken to skillet; add tomatoes, tomato paste, ginger, the remaining ½ teaspoon pepper blend, and the remaining ¼ teaspoon salt. Cook and stir just until heated through.

3. Meanwhile, cook spaghetti according to package directions; drain. Return spaghetti to the hot pan; stir in pesto.

4. Serve chicken and tomato mixture on top of pesto-coated spaghetti. If desired, top with shards of Parmesan cheese.

Per serving: 597 cal., 20 g total fat (2 g sat. fat), 84 mg chol., 641 mg sodium, 59 g carb., 4 g fiber, 44 g pro.

Ham and Turkey Club Burgers

These two-fisted burgers take the club sandwich to new heights—instead of sliced turkey, they feature grilled ham and turkey patties.

Prep: 15 minutes **Grill:** 10 minutes
Makes 4 servings

⅓ cup bottled dried tomato-flavored mayonnaise or Homemade Tomato Mayonnaise

¼ cup fine dry bread crumbs

¼ teaspoon ground black pepper

8 ounces ground cooked ham

8 ounces uncooked ground turkey

4 kaiser rolls or hamburger buns, split and toasted

1 large tomato, sliced

4 romaine leaves

4 slices bacon, crisp-cooked and halved

1. In a large bowl, combine 2 tablespoons of the tomato-flavored mayonnaise, the bread crumbs, and pepper. Add ham and turkey; mix well. Shape into four ½-inch-thick patties. Place patties on the rack of an uncovered grill directly over medium coals. Grill for 10 to 13 minutes or until done (165°F),* turning once halfway through grilling.

2. Spread cut sides of roll bottoms with remaining tomato-flavored mayonnaise. Serve patties in rolls with tomato slices, romaine leaves, and bacon.

Per serving: 487 cal., 22 g total fat (6 g sat. fat), 99 mg chol., 1,609 mg sodium, 40 g carb., 3 g fiber, 29 g pro.

Homemade Tomato Mayonnaise: In a small bowl, combine ⅓ cup mayonnaise and 1 to 2 tablespoons finely snipped drained oil-packed dried tomatoes.

*Test Kitchen Tip: The internal color of a burger is not a reliable doneness indicator. A turkey patty cooked to 165°F is safe, regardless of color. To measure the doneness of a patty, insert an instant-read thermometer through the side of the patty to a depth of 2 to 3 inches.

Apricot Turkey Steaks

These moist, tender turkey steaks get a double dose of fruit flavor from apricot nectar and apricot preserves.

Start to finish: 25 minutes
Makes 4 servings

1 6-ounce package chicken-flavored rice and vermicelli mix

2 turkey breast tenderloins (about 1¼ pounds total)

1 5½-ounce can apricot nectar

½ teaspoon salt

⅛ teaspoon ground cinnamon
Dash ground black pepper

3 tablespoons apricot preserves

1½ teaspoons cornstarch

1. Prepare rice mix according to package directions. Set aside.

2. Meanwhile, split each turkey breast tenderloin in half horizontally to make a total of four turkey steaks. In a large skillet, combine apricot nectar, salt, cinnamon, and pepper. Add turkey steaks. Bring to boiling; reduce heat. Cover and simmer about 10 minutes or until turkey is no longer pink (170°F).

3. Transfer turkey steaks to a serving platter, reserving cooking liquid in the skillet. Cover turkey and keep warm.

4. For sauce: In a small bowl, stir together apricot preserves and cornstarch; stir into reserved cooking liquid in the skillet. Cook and stir until thickened and bubbly. Cook and stir for 2 minutes more. Spoon rice mixture onto the serving platter. Pour some of the sauce over turkey; pass remaining sauce.

Per serving: 374 cal., 2 g total fat (1 g sat. fat), 88 mg chol., 1,054 mg sodium, 48 g carb., 1 g fiber, 39 g pro.

Hail, Caesar! That's what diners will be saying when they bite into these **scrumptious grilled turkey sandwiches** made with fluffy pita bread, lettuce, tomatoes, and Parmesan cheese.

Turkey Caesar Sandwiches

Turkey Caesar Sandwiches

No pita bread on hand? That's OK—use toasted kaiser or other rolls instead.

Prep: 10 minutes   **Grill:** 12 minutes
Makes 4 servings

- 2   **8-ounce turkey tenderloins or 4 skinless, boneless chicken breast halves**
- ½   **cup bottled Caesar salad dressing**
- 4   **teaspoons olive oil**
- ½   **teaspoon bottled minced garlic**
- 4   **thick pita bread rounds, split horizontally**
  Lettuce leaves
- 2   **medium tomatoes, sliced**
- 1   **medium avocado, peeled and sliced (optional)**
  Shaved Parmesan cheese

1. If using turkey breast tenderloins, split each in half horizontally. Place turkey or chicken on the rack of an uncovered grill directly over medium coals. Grill for 12 to 15 minutes or until turkey is tender and no longer pink, turning once. Set aside half of the salad dressing; brush remaining dressing on the turkey during the last 5 minutes of grilling.

2. Meanwhile, in a small bowl, stir together olive oil and garlic. Using a pastry brush, brush oil mixture over one side of *each* pita bread. Place pita bread, brushed sides down, on grill rack directly over medium coals. Grill 2 to 3 minutes or until toasted.

3. To assemble, cut turkey tenderloins crosswise into ½-inch-thick slices. Place lettuce leaves on grilled side of four of the pita bread halves. Top with tomato, turkey, and, if desired, avocado; drizzle with reserved salad dressing. Top with shaved Parmesan cheese. Top with remaining pita bread halves.

Per serving: 535 cal., 26 g total fat (5 g sat. fat), 74 mg chol., 823 mg sodium, 37 g carb., 2 g fiber, 36 g pro.

Brats with Onion-Pepper Relish

These slimmed-down brats give you all the flavor you expect with a lot fewer calories than the concession-stand variety.

Start to finish: 30 minutes
Makes 4 servings

- 4   **uncooked turkey bratwursts**
- ½   **cup water**
- 1   **small onion, thinly sliced**
- 1   **small red or green sweet pepper, cut into thin strips**
- ¼   **teaspoon ground black pepper**
- ⅛   **teaspoon salt**
- 2   **teaspoons butter or margarine**
- 4   **bratwurst buns, split and toasted**
- 3   **tablespoons spicy brown mustard**

1. In a large nonstick skillet, cook bratwursts over medium heat about 5 minutes or until brown, turning frequently. Carefully add the water. Bring to boiling; reduce heat. Cover and simmer for 15 to 20 minutes or until an instant-read meat thermometer inserted from the end of each bratwurst into the center registers 165°F. Drain on paper towels.

2. Meanwhile, in a covered medium saucepan, cook onion, sweet pepper, black pepper, and salt in hot butter for 3 minutes. Stir onion mixture. Cook, covered, for 3 to 4 minutes more or until onion is golden brown.

3. Spread cut sides of toasted buns with mustard. Serve bratwursts in buns topped with onion mixture.

Per serving: 284 cal., 12 g total fat (4 g sat. fat), 43 mg chol., 1,100 mg sodium, 27 g carb., 2 g fiber, 17 g pro.

Turkey Dinner Burgers

Turkey Dinner Burgers

For a colorful accompaniment, try a medley of vegetables cooked in the microwave and tossed with your favorite salad dressing.

Start to finish: 30 minutes
Makes 4 servings

- 1   **egg**
- ½   **teaspoon salt**
- ¼   **teaspoon ground black pepper**
- 1   **pound uncooked lean ground turkey or ground chicken**
- ¼   **cup fine dry bread crumbs**
- 1   **tablespoon olive oil**
- ¼   **cup jalapeño pepper jelly, melted, or bottled barbecue sauce**
-    **Thinly sliced red onion**
-    **Packaged shredded red cabbage**
- 4   **potato rolls, kaiser rolls, or hamburger buns, split and toasted**

1. In a large bowl, combine egg, salt, and black pepper; beat with a fork. Add turkey and bread crumbs; mix well. Shape the turkey mixture into four ¾-inch-thick patties.

2. In a large nonstick skillet, heat oil over medium heat. Add turkey patties; cook about 10 minutes or until done (165°F),* turning once halfway through grilling. Brush both sides of each patty with jalapeño jelly or barbecue sauce. To glaze, cook for 1 minute more on each side.

3. To assemble, place onion and cabbage on roll bottoms; top with turkey patties. Add roll tops.

Per serving: 504 cal., 20 g total fat (2 g sat. fat), 55 mg chol., 900 mg sodium, 52 g carb., 2 g fiber, 28 g pro.

*Test Kitchen Tip: The internal color of a burger is not a reliable doneness indicator. A turkey patty cooked to 165°F is safe, regardless of color. To measure the doneness of a patty, insert an instant-read thermometer through the side of the patty to a depth of 2 to 3 inches.

Beer-Chili Bean Soup

If you don't have any turkey leftovers, look for cooked turkey breast in your supermarket's meat department.

Start to finish: 20 minutes
Makes 4 servings

- 1   **15-ounce can hot-style chili beans with chili gravy**
- 1   **12-ounce can beer**
- 1   **11¼-ounce can condensed chili beef soup**
- 1½   **cups chopped cooked turkey (about 8 ounces)**
- 1   **cup hot water**
- 1   **teaspoon dried minced onion**
- 1   **teaspoon Worcestershire sauce**
- ½   **teaspoon garlic powder**
-    **Shredded cheddar cheese**
-    **Dairy sour cream (optional)**

1. In a large saucepan, combine chili beans with chili gravy, beer, chili beef soup, chopped turkey, the water, dried minced onion, Worcestershire sauce, and garlic powder.

2. Bring to boiling; reduce heat. Simmer, uncovered, for 5 minutes. Serve with cheese and, if desired, sour cream.

Per serving: 353 cal., 10 g total fat (5 g sat. fat), 57 mg chol., 1,154 mg sodium, 35 g carb., 12 g fiber, 27 g pro.

Choose Wisely

When you're shopping for uncooked ground poultry, keep in mind that some products can be quite high in fat because they include dark meat and skin. Always read product labels carefully. For the lowest-fat ground poultry, opt for ground turkey or chicken breast.

Apple Butter Chops

Kansas City and Montreal steak seasonings vary by manufacturers but typically include herbs, spices, peppers, and other seasonings that lend a barbecue flavor to foods.

Prep: 10 minutes **Grill:** 11 minutes
Makes 4 servings

4 pork loin or rib chops, cut ¾ inch thick
½ teaspoon Kansas City or Montreal steak seasoning
½ cup bottled chili sauce
¼ cup apple butter
½ teaspoon apple pie spice, pumpkin pie spice, or ground cinnamon
2 medium zucchini and/or yellow summer squash, halved lengthwise

1. Sprinkle pork chops lightly with steak seasoning. For sauce: In a small bowl, combine chili sauce, apple butter, and apple pie spice; set aside.

2. Place chops and zucchini on the rack of an uncovered grill directly over medium coals. Grill for 11 to 14 minutes or until chops are slightly pink in the center and juices run clear (160°F) and the zucchini is tender, turning once and brushing chops and zucchini with the sauce during the last 3 minutes of grilling.
Per serving: 378 cal., 9 g total fat (3 g sat. fat), 110 mg chol., 622 mg sodium, 33 g carb., 4 g fiber, 39 g pro.

Food Safety Tips

It's important to make sure the surface of the food is cooked before adding brush-on sauces and glazes to grilled or broiled meat, poultry, or fish. This keeps the mixture from coming in contact with raw food, which may contain harmful bacteria. If you do use a sauce or glaze earlier in the cooking process, be sure to stop brushing during the last half of grilling or broiling. Also, discard any remaining sauce or glaze mixture.

Canadian Bacon Pizza

This fast-grilling entrée puts all of the sizzle and smoke you love into one of the world's most popular treats. Purchased Italian bread shells make the recipe a real snap to prepare.

Prep: 20 minutes **Grill:** 5 minutes
Makes 4 servings

1 6-ounce jar marinated artichoke hearts, quartered
2 6-inch Italian bread shells (such as Boboli brand)
1 cup shredded fontina or mozzarella cheese (4 ounces)
6 slices Canadian-style bacon, cut into strips (about 5 ounces)
3 plum tomatoes, sliced
¼ cup crumbled feta cheese (1 ounce)
2 green onions, thinly sliced
1 tablespoon snipped fresh oregano or basil

1. Drain artichoke hearts, reserving marinade. Brush the bread shells with some of the reserved marinade (discard any remaining marinade). Sprinkle half of the fontina cheese over bread shells. In a large bowl, toss together artichoke hearts, Canadian-style bacon, tomatoes, feta cheese, green onions, and oregano; divide among bread shells. Sprinkle with the remaining fontina cheese.

2. Transfer the bread shells to a pizza grill pan or a large piece of double-thickness heavy foil. On a grill that has a cover, place the pan or foil on the rack of the grill directly over medium coals. Cover and grill for 5 to 8 minutes or until cheese is melted and pizza is heated through.
Per serving: 384 cal., 19 g total fat (7 g sat. fat), 58 mg chol., 1,246 mg sodium, 33 g carb., 1 g fiber, 23 g pro.

Canadian Bacon Pizza

White Beans and Spinach Ragout

Diced tomatoes, white kidney beans, fresh spinach, and a **drizzle of balsamic vinaigrette** make this tricolor combination as tasty as it is **eye-catching.**

White Beans and Spinach Ragout

White kidney beans were originally developed in Italy and are sometimes called by their Italian name, cannellini beans. You'll find them with the other beans in most large supermarkets.

Start to finish: 20 minutes
Makes 3 servings

 1   **14½-ounce can diced tomatoes**
 2   **slices bacon, cut into 1-inch pieces**
 1   **medium onion, halved and thinly sliced**
 1   **15-ounce can white kidney beans (cannellini beans) or navy beans, rinsed and drained**
 4   **cups torn fresh spinach**
 4   **teaspoons bottled balsamic or red wine vinaigrette salad dressing**

1. Drain tomatoes, reserving ⅓ cup of the liquid; set aside. In a large skillet, cook bacon pieces over medium heat until crisp. Remove with slotted spoon, reserving 1 tablespoon of the drippings in skillet. Drain bacon on paper towels.

2. Add onion to bacon drippings in skillet; cook about 3 minutes or just until tender. Stir in beans, tomatoes, and reserved tomato liquid. Cook and stir over medium heat about 2 minutes or until heated through. Stir in 3 cups of the spinach; cover and cook about 30 seconds or just until wilted. Stir in cooked bacon and the remaining 1 cup spinach. Drizzle individual servings with vinaigrette.

Per serving: 221 cal., 9 g total fat (3 g sat. fat), 10 mg chol., 678 mg sodium, 31 g carb., 8 g fiber, 12 g pro.

Pork and Apples

For wedges that keep their shape as they cook, make this spicy-sweet medley with Rome Beauty or York Imperial apples.

Start to finish: 30 minutes
Makes 4 servings

 1   **12-ounce pork tenderloin**
 ¼   **teaspoon salt**
 ¼   **teaspoon ground black pepper**
 5   **teaspoons olive oil**
 1   **large red onion, halved and sliced**
 ¾   **cup apple juice or apple cider**
 2   **tablespoons red wine vinegar**
 1   **tablespoon spicy brown mustard**
 2   **medium cooking apples, cut into wedges**
 1   **teaspoon snipped fresh rosemary or ½ teaspoon dried rosemary, crushed**

1. Cut tenderloin crosswise into ½-inch-thick slices; sprinkle with salt and pepper.

2. In a 12-inch skillet, heat 3 teaspoons of the oil over medium heat. Add pork slices; cook for 6 to 8 minutes or until done (160°F), turning once. Remove pork slices from skillet.

3. Add the remaining 2 teaspoons oil and the onion to skillet. Cook and stir for 2 minutes. Carefully stir in apple juice, red wine vinegar, and mustard. Bring to boiling; reduce heat.

4. Add apple wedges and rosemary to skillet. Cook about 4 minutes or just until apple wedges are tender and most of the liquid has evaporated. Add the pork slices; heat through.

Per serving: 225 cal., 9 g total fat (2 g sat. fat), 55 mg chol., 240 mg sodium, 18 g carb., 2 g fiber, 19 g pro.

Barley and Bean Skillet

If you have a few extra minutes, you can shred your own carrot instead of using the preshredded kind.

Start to finish: 30 minutes
Makes 4 servings

1	**14-ounce can vegetable broth**
⅓	**cup water**
1¼	**cups quick-cooking barley**
2	**cups loose-pack frozen cut green beans**
1	**10¾-ounce can condensed cream of onion soup**
½	**cup purchased shredded carrot**
½	**cup milk**
½	**teaspoon dried thyme, crushed**
1	**cup shredded sharp cheddar cheese (4 ounces)**

1. In a large skillet, combine vegetable broth and the water; bring to boiling. Stir in barley. Return to boiling; reduce heat. Cover and simmer for 5 minutes.

2. Stir in green beans, cream of onion soup, carrot, milk, and thyme. Bring to boiling; reduce heat. Cover and simmer for 12 to 15 minutes more or until barley is tender and most of the liquid is absorbed, stirring occasionally. Stir in half of the cheese.

3. Sprinkle with the remaining cheese. Let stand for 2 to 3 minutes or until cheese is melted.

Per serving: 394 cal., 15 g total fat (8 g sat. fat), 45 mg chol., 1,193 mg sodium, 52 g carb., 8 g fiber, 16 g pro.

Dinner on the Double

One-dish meals, such as meatless Barley and Bean Skillet and Chunky Chipotle Pork Chile, are great time-savers—all you have to add is a tossed or fruit salad and dinner's done. Keep ice cream and cookies on hand for anyone who wants to top off the meal with a sweet ending.

Chunky Chipotle Pork Chili

For an extra burst of tongue-tingling flavor, use the 2 tablespoons chipotle chile peppers.

Start to finish: 30 minutes
Makes 4 servings

1	**tablespoon cooking oil**
1	**small onion, chopped**
2	**teaspoons bottled minced garlic**
12	**ounces pork tenderloin, cut into ¾-inch cubes**
2	**teaspoons chili powder**
2	**teaspoons ground cumin**
1	**yellow or red sweet pepper, cut into ½-inch pieces**
1	**cup beer or beef broth**
½	**cup bottled picante sauce or salsa**
1	**to 2 tablespoons finely chopped canned chipotle chile peppers in adobo sauce (see tip, page 58)**
1	**15-ounce can small red beans or pinto beans, rinsed and drained**
½	**cup dairy sour cream**
	Fresh cilantro or flat-leaf parsley sprigs (optional)

1. In a large saucepan, heat oil over medium-high heat. Add onion and garlic; cook about 3 minutes or until tender.

2. In a medium bowl, toss pork with chili powder and cumin; add to saucepan. Cook and stir until pork is browned. Add sweet pepper, beer or beef broth, picante sauce or salsa, and chipotle chile peppers. Bring to boiling; reduce heat. Cover and simmer about 5 minutes or until pork is tender. Stir in beans; heat through. Top individual servings with sour cream. If desired, garnish with cilantro or parsley.

Per serving: 328 cal., 11 g total fat (4 g sat. fat), 65 mg chol., 625 mg sodium, 29 g carb., 7 g fiber, 26 g pro.

Even though lean pork tenderloin **cooks to perfection in just minutes,** this down-home stew gets a rich, **simmered-all-day flavor** from chipotle chile peppers.

Chunky Chipotle Pork Chili

The barbecue sauce of choice for **grilled chops** varies with the part of the country you're in. This Southern-style recipe relies on **chili sauce and molasses** rather than ketchup.

Memphis-Style Pork Chops

Memphis-Style Pork Chops

Stop by your favorite deli or supermarket to pick up coleslaw or potato salad to go along with these fork-tender chops.

Prep: 15 minutes **Grill:** 12 minutes
Makes 4 servings

½	cup bottled chili sauce
2	tablespoons molasses
2	tablespoons cider vinegar
1	teaspoon chili powder
4	boneless pork loin chops, cut ¾ to 1 inch thick (about 1¼ pounds total)
1	teaspoon dried basil, crushed
½	teaspoon paprika
¼	teaspoon salt
¼	teaspoon onion powder
¼	teaspoon cayenne pepper

1. In a small saucepan, stir together chili sauce, molasses, vinegar, and chili powder. Bring to boiling; reduce heat. Simmer, uncovered, for 3 minutes. Remove from heat.

2. Trim fat from chops. In a small bowl, stir together basil, paprika, salt, onion powder, and cayenne pepper. Sprinkle evenly over both sides of each chop; rub in with your fingers.

3. Place chops on the rack of an uncovered grill directly over medium coals. Grill for 12 to 15 minutes or until juices run clear (160°F), turning once and brushing with chili sauce mixture during the last 5 minutes of grilling.

Per serving: 260 cal., 7 g total fat (3 g sat. fat), 83 mg chol., 623 mg sodium, 16 g carb., 2 g fiber, 31 g pro.

Tuna Alfredo Casserole

This easy-fixin' main dish offers weeknight convenience, Sunday night comfort, and anytime taste. Feel free to substitute any pesto you please.

Prep: 20 minutes **Bake:** 10 minutes
Oven: 425°F
Makes 6 servings

3	cups dried rigatoni or penne pasta
2	tablespoons purchased dried tomato pesto
1	10-ounce container refrigerated Alfredo or four-cheese pasta sauce, or 1¼ cups bottled Alfredo or four-cheese pasta sauce
3	tablespoons milk
1	12-ounce can water-packed solid white tuna, drained and broken into chunks
¼	cup finely shredded Parmesan cheese (1 ounce)

1. Preheat oven to 425°F. In a Dutch oven, cook pasta according to package directions. Drain well. Return pasta to hot pan; cover to keep warm.

2. Meanwhile, in a medium bowl, combine pesto, Alfredo sauce, and milk. Add pesto mixture to pasta, stirring gently to coat. Gently fold in tuna.

3. Transfer pasta mixture to a 2-quart oval baking dish. Sprinkle with shredded Parmesan cheese. Bake for 10 to 15 minutes or until heated through and cheese is just melted.

Per serving: 453 cal., 24 g total fat (4 g sat. fat), 53 mg chol., 587 mg sodium, 35 g carb., 2 g fiber, 24 g pro.

Red Beans and Orzo

A takeoff on **old-fashioned Southern red beans and rice,** this easy-fixing skillet dish substitutes tiny orzo pasta for the rice.

Red Beans and Orzo

Herbes de Provence, a seasoning blend used in the Provence region of France, often includes basil, fennel, lavender, marjoram, rosemary, sage, savory, and thyme. If you don't have any on your spice shelf, Italian seasoning makes a tasty substitute.

Start to finish: 30 minutes
Makes 4 servings

1	14-ounce can chicken broth
1½	cups water
1⅓	cups dried orzo pasta (rosamarina)
¼	cup finely chopped onion
1	teaspoon herbes de Provence or dried Italian seasoning, crushed
1	15-ounce can red beans or pinto beans, rinsed and drained
1	ounce prosciutto or cooked ham, cut into thin strips (about ⅓ cup)
2	tablespoons snipped fresh flat-leaf parsley
⅓	cup finely shredded Parmesan cheese

1. In a medium saucepan, combine broth and the water; bring to boiling. Stir in uncooked orzo, onion, and herbes de Provence. Return to boiling; reduce heat. Simmer, uncovered, for 12 to 15 minutes or just until orzo is tender and most of the liquid is absorbed, stirring often.

2. Stir in drained beans, prosciutto or ham, and parsley; heat through. Top individual servings with Parmesan cheese.

Per serving: 350 cal., 4 g total fat (1 g sat. fat), 11 mg chol., 1,118 mg sodium, 61 g carb., 7 g fiber, 18 g pro.

Salmon Confetti Chowder

If watercress isn't available, use snipped fresh parsley, spinach, or basil.

Start to finish: 25 minutes
Makes 4 servings

2	cups frozen (yellow, green, and red) pepper and onion stir-fry vegetables
2	tablespoons minced seeded fresh jalapeño chile peppers (see tip, page 58)
1	tablespoon butter or margarine
2	tablespoons all-purpose flour
2	cups milk
1	cup half-and-half or light cream
2	cups refrigerated diced potatoes with onions
1	15-ounce can salmon, drained and flaked
¼	cup snipped fresh watercress
½	teaspoon finely shredded lemon peel
½	teaspoon salt
½	teaspoon ground black pepper

1. In a large saucepan, cook stir-fry vegetables and chile peppers in hot butter for 3 to 5 minutes or until tender. Stir in flour. Stir in milk and half-and-half. Cook and stir until slightly thickened. Cook and stir for 2 minutes more.

2. Stir in diced potatoes, salmon, watercress, shredded lemon peel, salt, and black pepper. Cook and stir until chowder is heated through.

Per serving: 410 cal., 17 g total fat (8 g sat. fat), 40 mg chol., 531 mg sodium, 30 g carb., 3 g fiber, 34 g pro.

Salmon-Sauced English Muffins

Although this recipe makes a sensational weeknight supper, you can also enjoy it for brunch.

Start to finish: 20 minutes
Makes 4 servings

1	10-ounce container refrigerated Alfredo pasta sauce
1	9- to 10-ounce package frozen cut asparagus, thawed
1	4-ounce can (drained weight) mushroom stems and pieces, drained
1	teaspoon lemon juice
¼	teaspoon dried dill
1	6-ounce can skinless, boneless salmon, drained and flaked
1	tablespoon dry sherry
4	English muffins, split and toasted

1. In a medium saucepan, combine Alfredo pasta sauce, thawed asparagus, mushrooms, lemon juice, and dill. Cook and stir over medium heat until bubbly and heated through. Remove from heat; stir in salmon and sherry.

2. Spoon salmon mixture over English muffin halves.

Per serving: 440 cal., 25 g total fat (0 g sat. fat), 35 mg chol., 636 mg sodium, 34 g carb., 3 g fiber, 20 g pro.

Canned Mushroom Weight

Labels can sometimes be confusing. If you read the labels on canned or bottled mushrooms, you'll find they list drained weight rather than the weight with liquid. This differs from many other canned products that list the total weight. Because canned and bottled mushrooms actually do contain liquid, they usually need to be drained before using. Read the wording of recipes carefully.

Salmon with Feta and Pasta

Feta, the world's favorite Greek cheese, shares its tangy flavor with fish in this colorful combo.

Start to finish: 25 minutes
Makes 5 servings

12	ounces fresh or frozen skinless salmon fillet
8	ounces dried rotini pasta
	Nonstick cooking spray
1	teaspoon bottled minced garlic
	Salt
4	large plum tomatoes, chopped (2 cups)
1	cup sliced green onions
⅓	cup sliced pitted ripe olives
3	tablespoons snipped fresh basil
½	teaspoon coarsely ground black pepper
2	teaspoons olive oil
1	4-ounce package crumbled feta cheese
	Fresh basil sprigs (optional)

1. Thaw fish, if frozen. Rinse fish; pat dry with paper towels. Cut into 1-inch pieces. Cook pasta according to package directions. Drain well. Return pasta to hot pan; cover to keep warm.

2. Meanwhile, lightly coat an unheated large nonstick skillet with nonstick cooking spray. Preheat skillet over medium-high heat. Add garlic. Cook and stir for 15 seconds. Lightly season fish pieces with salt. Add fish to skillet. Cook fish for 4 to 6 minutes or until fish flakes easily when tested with a fork, turning fish pieces occasionally. Stir in tomatoes, green onions, olives, basil, and pepper. Heat through.

3. In a large bowl, toss together hot pasta and olive oil. Add salmon mixture and feta cheese; toss gently. If desired, garnish with basil sprigs.

Per serving: 373 cal., 13 g total fat (5 g sat. fat), 56 mg chol., 443 mg sodium, 41 g carb., 3 g fiber, 24 g pro.

Salmon with Feta and Pasta

Sole with Caponata

Sole with Caponata

Zesty caponata (the Italian cousin of France's ratatouille) turns ordinary fish into a fresh and lively dinner. Another time, try the caponata on your favorite sandwich or use it to top broiled chicken.

Start to finish: 20 minutes
Makes 4 servings

4	**4-ounce fresh or frozen skinless sole fillets**
1	**14½-ounce can Italian-style stewed tomatoes, undrained**
2	**tablespoons olive oil**
2	**cups chopped, peeled eggplant**
1	**small yellow, green, or red sweet pepper, coarsely chopped**
¼	**cup bottled picante sauce**
½	**teaspoon bottled minced garlic**
1	**tablespoon balsamic vinegar**
⅛	**teaspoon salt**
⅛	**teaspoon ground black pepper**
	Lemon wedges (optional)

1. Thaw fish fillets, if frozen. Rinse fish; pat dry with paper towels.

2. For caponata: Cut up any large tomato pieces; set aside. In a large nonstick skillet, heat 1 tablespoon of the oil over medium-high heat. Add eggplant; cook about 3 minutes or until golden brown, stirring occasionally. Stir in undrained tomatoes, sweet pepper, picante sauce, and garlic. Bring to boiling; reduce heat. Simmer, uncovered, for 4 to 5 minutes or until slightly thickened. Stir in balsamic vinegar. Remove from skillet; set aside.

3. Wipe out skillet with paper towels. Sprinkle fish with the salt and pepper. In the same skillet, heat the remaining 1 tablespoon oil over medium heat. Add fish; cook for 4 to 6 minutes or until fish flakes easily when tested with a fork. Serve caponata with fish. If desired, garnish with lemon wedges.

Per serving: 225 cal., 9 g total fat (1 g sat. fat), 49 mg chol., 481 mg sodium, 13 g carb., 3 g fiber, 22 g pro.

Oven-Fried Fish

No need to haul out the skillet to enjoy fried fish. This version bakes in as little as 4 minutes. What's more, there are no messy cooking oil splatters to clean up.

Prep: 15 minutes
Bake: 4 minutes per ½-inch thickness
Oven: 450°F
Makes 4 servings

1	**pound fresh or frozen skinless cod, orange roughy, or catfish fillets**
¼	**cup milk**
⅓	**cup all-purpose flour**
½	**cup fine dry bread crumbs**
2	**tablespoons grated Parmesan cheese**
¼	**teaspoon lemon-pepper seasoning**
2	**tablespoons butter or margarine, melted**
	Lemon wedges (optional)

1. Preheat oven to 450°F. Thaw fish, if frozen. Rinse fish; pat dry with paper towels. If necessary, cut into four serving-size pieces. Measure the thickness of each piece. Place milk in a shallow dish. Place flour in another shallow dish. In a third shallow dish, combine bread crumbs, Parmesan cheese, and lemon-pepper seasoning. Add melted butter to bread crumb mixture; stir until well mixed.

2. Grease a shallow baking pan; set aside. Dip fish in the milk; coat with flour. Dip again in the milk; dip in the crumb mixture, turning to coat all sides. Place fish in a single layer in prepared baking pan. Bake, uncovered, for 4 to 6 minutes per ½-inch thickness or until fish flakes easily when tested with a fork. If desired, serve with lemon wedges.

Per serving: 254 cal., 9 g total fat (5 g sat. fat), 75 mg chol., 565 mg sodium, 15 g carb., 1 g fiber, 26 g pro.

Fish Fillets with Salsa Verde

When you're pressed for time, fish fillets broil in just a few minutes. Top the fish with a lively mixture of bottled green salsa and snipped cilantro.

Prep: 10 minutes   **Broil:** 4 minutes per ½-inch thickness
Makes 4 servings

1	pound fresh or frozen cod or orange roughy fillets
1	medium lime
1	tablespoon olive oil
⅛	teaspoon salt
⅛	teaspoon ground black pepper
½	cup bottled green salsa
3	tablespoons snipped fresh cilantro

1. Thaw fish, if frozen. Rinse fish; pat dry with paper towels. Cut lime in half; squeeze to get 1 tablespoon juice. Cut remaining lime half into wedges; set wedges aside. In a small bowl combine lime juice, oil, salt, and pepper. Brush fish with lime juice mixture.

2. Preheat broiler. Measure thickness of fish. Place fish on the greased unheated rack of a broiler pan. Tuck under any thin edges. Broil 4 inches from heat until fish flakes easily when tested with a fork. (Allow 4 to 6 minutes per ½-inch thickness of fish. If fillets are 1 inch thick, turn once halfway through broiling.)

3. Meanwhile, stir together green salsa and 2 tablespoons of the cilantro. Top fish with salsa mixture; sprinkle with the remaining 1 tablespoon cilantro. Serve with reserved lime wedges.

Per serving: 125 cal., 4 g total fat (1 g sat. fat), 42 mg chol., 157 mg sodium, 1 g carbo., 0 g fiber, 20 g pro.

Salsa, Bean, and Cheese Pizza

No need to fuss with making a crust; this Tex-Mex pizza uses corn tortillas instead.

Start to finish: 20 minutes   **Oven:** 425°F
Makes 4 servings

4	6-inch corn tortillas
4	teaspoons olive oil
1	medium onion, chopped (½ cup)
1	fresh jalapeño chile pepper, seeded and finely chopped*
1	clove garlic, minced
1	cup rinsed and drained canned black beans
1	cup chopped seeded tomato
4	ounces Monterey Jack, cheddar, or mozzarella cheese, shredded (1 cup)
2	tablespoons chopped fresh cilantro

1. Preheat oven to 425°F. Place tortillas on an ungreased baking sheet. Lightly brush tortillas on both sides with 1 teaspoon of the oil. Bake about 3 minutes on each side until lightly browned and crisp.

2. Meanwhile, in a large skillet, cook onion, chile pepper, and garlic in the remaining 3 teaspoons oil over medium-high heat until onion is tender. Stir in black beans and tomato; heat through.

3. Sprinkle tortillas with half of the cheese. Spoon bean mixture over cheese. Sprinkle with remaining cheese. Bake about 4 minutes or until cheese melts. Sprinkle with cilantro.

Per serving: 231 cal., 11 g total fat (4 g sat. fat), 20 mg chol., 496 mg sodium, 25 g carbo., 6 g fiber, 12 g pro.

*Test Kitchen Tip: Because chile peppers contain volatile oils that can burn your skin and eyes, avoid direct contact with them as much as possible. When working with chile peppers, wear plastic or rubber gloves. If your bare hands do touch the peppers, wash your hands and nails well with soap and warm water.

Salsa, Bean, and Cheese Pizza

Get off that same old mustard, pickle, and ketchup merry-go-round with these **grilled meatless burgers** that feature an **irresistibly tangy spinach-feta topper.**

Garden Veggie Burgers

Garden Veggie Burgers

To toast the hamburger buns, place them on the edge of the grill for a few minutes while the burgers cook.
Prep: 10 minutes   **Grill:** 15 minutes
Makes 4 servings

2	medium red onions, cut into ½-inch-thick slices
4	refrigerated or frozen meatless burger patties
¼	cup bottled vinaigrette salad dressing (at room temperature)
1	tablespoon olive oil
4	cups fresh spinach leaves
½	teaspoon bottled minced garlic
½	cup crumbled feta cheese (2 ounces)
4	hamburger buns, split and toasted

1. Place onion slices on the rack of an uncovered grill directly over medium coals. Grill for 15 to 20 minutes or until tender, turning once. Grill burger patties directly over the coals alongside the onions for 8 to 10 minutes or until heated through, turning once halfway through grilling. Brush grilled onions with the vinaigrette salad dressing.

2. Meanwhile, for spinach topping: In a large skillet, heat olive oil over medium-high heat. Add spinach and garlic; cook about 30 seconds or just until spinach is wilted. Remove from heat. Stir in the crumbled feta cheese.

3. To serve, divide grilled onions among bun bottoms. Top with grilled burger patties, spinach topping, and bun tops.
Per serving: 350 cal., 14 g total fat (4 g sat. fat), 17 mg chol., 920 mg sodium, 37 g carb., 7 g fiber, 21 g pro.

Bean and Cheese Quesadillas

These full-of-veggies quesadillas are quick, colorful, and tasty. The diced peaches add a hint of sweetness.
Prep: 15 minutes   **Bake:** 12 minutes
Oven: 400°F
Makes 4 servings

½	of a 16-ounce can (¾ cup) refried beans
1	8-ounce can whole kernel corn, drained
¼	cup purchased salsa
1	canned chipotle chile pepper in adobo sauce, drained and chopped (see tip, page 58) (optional)
8	8-inch flour tortillas
2	tablespoons cooking oil
1	cup packaged shredded broccoli (broccoli slaw mix)
1	4- to 4¼-ounce can or container diced peaches, drained
1	cup finely shredded Mexican cheese blend (4 ounces)
	Purchased guacamole dip, dairy sour cream, and/or purchased salsa

1. Preheat oven to 400°F. In a small bowl, combine refried beans, corn, the ¼ cup salsa, and, if desired, chile pepper. Brush one side of each tortilla with some of the oil. Spread bean mixture over the unoiled sides of four of the tortillas; set aside.

2. In another small bowl, combine broccoli and peaches. Top bean mixture on tortillas with broccoli mixture. Top with cheese. Top with remaining tortillas, oiled sides up; press down lightly. Place on a large baking sheet.

3. Bake for 12 to 15 minutes or until golden brown and cheese is melted. Serve with guacamole dip, sour cream, and/or additional salsa.
Per serving: 444 cal., 21 g total fat (7 g sat. fat), 25 mg chol., 825 mg sodium, 50 g carb., 5 g fiber, 14 g pro.

Asian Chicken Salad

take 5
ingredients

You don't need a cart full of groceries to create any of these tantalizing main-dish recipes. Each one relies on five or fewer ingredients for its fabulous flavor. Choose from an enticing array of speedy meat, poultry, fish, and meatless ideas.

Asian Chicken Salad

When you need something quick for lunch or dinner, this salad is it. The dressing and oranges add a distinctly Asian flavor to ready-to-use torn salad greens.

Start to finish: 15 minutes
Makes 4 servings

1 **10-ounce package torn mixed salad greens**
8 **ounces cooked chicken, cut into bite-size pieces**
⅓ **cup bottled Asian vinaigrette salad dressing**
1 **11-ounce can mandarin orange sections, drained**
3 **tablespoons sliced almonds, toasted**

1. In a large bowl, combine greens and chicken. Add vinaigrette salad dressing; toss to coat. Divide greens mixture among four salad plates. Top with mandarin orange sections and almonds. Serve immediately.

Per serving: 218 cal., 9 g total fat (1 g sat. fat), 50 mg chol., 502 mg sodium, 15 g carb., 2 g fiber, 19 g pro.

What Counts?

The ingredients used in the no-fuss recipes in this chapter are ones you easily can find in most supermarkets. To calculate the five ingredients for each recipe, optional ingredients, water, and shelf-stable pantry staples—salt, pepper, nonstick cooking spray, and cooking oil—were omitted.

Mock Monte Cristo Sandwiches

Starting with frozen French toast eliminates the need to fry these turkey-and-ham-filled "cheesewiches." They just bake in the oven for a few minutes.

Prep: 10 minutes **Bake:** 15 minutes
Oven: 400°F
Makes 6 half sandwiches

6   **slices frozen French toast**
2   **tablespoons honey mustard**
3   **ounces sliced cooked turkey breast**
3   **ounces sliced cooked ham**
3   **ounces thinly sliced Swiss cheese**

1. Preheat oven to 400°F. Lightly grease a baking sheet; set aside. To assemble sandwiches, spread one side of each of the frozen French toast slices with honey mustard. Layer three of the French toast slices, mustard sides up, with the sliced turkey, ham, and cheese. Cover with remaining French toast slices, mustard sides down.

2. Place sandwiches on prepared baking sheet. Bake for 15 to 20 minutes or until sandwiches are heated through, turning sandwiches over once. Cut each sandwich in half diagonally.

Per half sandwich: 221 cal., 9 g total fat (4 g sat. fat), 75 mg chol., 704 mg sodium, 21 g carb., 1 g fiber, 14 g pro.

Mix-and-Match Sandwiches

Don't have sliced cooked turkey and ham and Swiss cheese for Mock Monte Cristo Sandwiches? Be creative—use whatever cooked meat and cheese combination you have on hand. How about roast beef with salami and cheddar cheese? Or try chicken with Monterey Jack cheese with jalapeño chile peppers. These versatile sandwiches will taste great with almost any combo you choose.

Two-Step Crunchy Chicken Strips

Coating and baking the uncooked chicken breast tenderloins give you plump, crunchy chicken strips in 20 minutes. For an even speedier version, start with cooked chicken breast strips from the refrigerated meat or deli case. Dip and coat them as directed and reheat in the oven for about 5 minutes.

Prep: 10 minutes **Bake:** 10 minutes
Oven: 425°F
Makes 4 to 6 servings

      Nonstick cooking spray
2½   **cups crushed bite-size cheddar fish-shape crackers and/or pretzels**
⅔   **cup bottled buttermilk ranch salad dressing or honey Dijon-style mustard**
1   **pound chicken breast tenderloins**
      Bottled buttermilk ranch salad dressing or honey Dijon-style mustard (optional)

1. Preheat oven to 425°F. Line a 15×10×1-inch baking pan with foil; lightly coat foil with nonstick cooking spray. Set aside. Place crushed crackers in a shallow dish. Place the ⅔ cup ranch dressing or mustard in another shallow dish. Dip chicken tenderloins into the dressing or mustard, allowing excess to drip off; dip into crushed crackers to coat. Arrange chicken in prepared pan.

2. Bake for 10 to 15 minutes or until chicken is tender and no longer pink. If desired, serve with additional ranch dressing or mustard.

Per serving: 517 cal., 21 g total fat (2 g sat. fat), 66 mg chol., 1,060 mg sodium, 51 g carb., 2 g fiber, 33 g pro.

Two-Step Crunchy Chicken Strips

Stuffed Focaccia

Mascarpone cheese, artichoke hearts, salami, and arugula layered in focaccia add up to one tremendous sandwich.

Start to finish: 20 minutes
Makes 3 servings

½ of a 9- to 10-inch garlic, onion, or plain Italian flat bread (focaccia), split horizontally

½ of an 8-ounce container mascarpone cheese

1 6-ounce jar marinated artichoke hearts, drained and chopped

4 ounces thinly sliced Genoa salami

1 cup arugula leaves

1. Spread cut sides of focaccia with mascarpone cheese. Sprinkle bottom half of focaccia with artichoke hearts; top with salami and arugula leaves. Add top of focaccia, spread side down.

2. Cut sandwich into thirds. Serve immediately or chill up to 4 hours before serving.

Per serving: 545 cal., 36 g total fat (16 g sat. fat), 83 mg chol., 970 mg sodium, 43 g carbo., 3 g fiber, 23 g pro.

Chicken Focaccia Sandwiches

For easy slicing, purchase a flatbread that is about 1 inch thick. That thickness also provides the perfect proportion of chewy bread to savory filling.
Start to finish: 15 minutes
Makes 4 servings

1	8- to 10-inch tomato or onion Italian flatbread (focaccia) or 1 loaf sourdough bread
⅓	cup light mayonnaise dressing or salad dressing
1	cup lightly packed fresh basil
1½	cups sliced or shredded deli-roasted chicken
½	of a 7-ounce jar roasted red sweet peppers, drained and cut into strips (about ½ cup)

1. Using a long serrated knife, cut bread in half horizontally. Spread cut sides of bread halves with mayonnaise dressing.

2. Layer basil leaves, chicken, and roasted sweet peppers between bread halves. Cut into quarters.
Per serving: 314 cal., 10 g total fat (1 g sat. fat), 40 mg chol., 597 mg sodium, 40 g carbo., 1 g fiber, 19 g pro.

Apple-Dijon Chicken

These butterflied chicken breasts cook quickly in hot butter. Choose large chicken breast halves so you can butterfly them easily.
Start to finish: 30 minutes
Makes 4 servings

4	large skinless, boneless chicken breast halves (about 1½ pounds)
	Salt and black pepper
2	tablespoons butter
1	medium tart cooking apple (such as Granny Smith), thinly sliced
⅓	cup whipping cream
2	tablespoons Dijon-style mustard

1. Butterfly cut each chicken breast half by cutting horizontally from one long side of the breast almost to, but not through, the opposite long side of the breast. Lay the breast open. Sprinkle both sides of chicken breasts with salt and pepper.

2. In a large skillet cook chicken, half at a time, in 1 tablespoon of the butter over medium-high heat until no longer pink (170°F), turning to brown evenly, about 2 to 3 minutes per side. Remove from skillet; keep warm.

3. Add remaining 1 tablespoon butter to skillet. Add sliced apple; cook and stir 3 minutes or until tender. Add whipping cream and mustard to skillet. Cook and stir until heated through and thickened slightly. Season to taste with additional salt and pepper. Serve sauce and apples over chicken.
Per serving: 342 cal., 16 g total fat (9 g sat. fat), 142 mg chol., 407 mg sodium, 6 g carbo., 1 g fiber, 40 g pro.

Tortellini and Cheese

Maple-Pecan Glazed Pork Chops

Deliciously gooey, these succulent chops boast a captivating blend of maple and pecan flavors.

Start to finish: 15 minutes
Makes 4 servings

- 4   boneless pork loin chops, about ¾ inch thick (about 1 pound total)
- 4   tablespoons butter or margarine, softened
- 2   tablespoons maple-flavored syrup
- ⅓   cup chopped pecans, toasted

1. Sprinkle chops with salt and ground black pepper. In a 12-inch skillet, melt 1 tablespoon of the butter over medium-high heat. Add chops; cook for 9 to 13 minutes or until pork juices run clear (160°F), turning once halfway through cooking. Transfer chops to a serving platter.

2. Meanwhile, in a small bowl, stir together the remaining 3 tablespoons butter and the maple syrup. Spread butter mixture evenly over chops. Let stand about 1 minute or until melted. Sprinkle with toasted pecans.

Per serving: 333 cal., 23 g total fat (10 g sat. fat), 98 mg chol., 310 mg sodium, 8 g carb., 1 g fiber, 23 g pro.

Tortellini and Cheese

Boiling the water is the most time-consuming part of making this superfast spin on mac and cheese.

Start to finish: 20 minutes
Makes 4 servings

- 1   9-ounce package refrigerated cheese tortellini
- 1   cup loose-pack frozen peas, corn, or pea pods
- 1   8-ounce tub cream cheese spread with garden vegetables or chive and onion
- ½   cup milk
- 1   9-ounce package frozen chopped cooked chicken breast

1. Cook tortellini according to package directions. Place frozen vegetables in colander. Drain hot pasta over vegetables to thaw; return pasta-vegetable mixture to hot pan.

2. Meanwhile, in a small saucepan, combine cream cheese and milk; heat and stir until cheese is melted. Heat chicken according to package directions.

3. Stir cream cheese mixture into cooked pasta-vegetable mixture. Cook and gently stir until heated through. Spoon into individual serving bowls. Top with chicken.

Per serving: 505 cal., 26 g total fat (15 g sat. fat), 130 mg chol., 525 mg sodium, 32 g carb., 2 g fiber, 32 g pro.

Stock Up

Keep frozen chopped cooked chicken breast on hand— it's great for all types of fast-fixin' main dishes. Include it in a chef's salad, sprinkle it over frozen cheese pizza, stir it into canned soup, or add it to spaghetti sauce to serve over pasta. The tempting possibilities are endless.

Roast Beef and Mashed Potato Stacks

Imagine a comforting meat and potatoes dinner in 15 minutes. Thanks to precooked beef tips and ready-to-go mashed potatoes, all you have to do is add a few ingredients and dinner is ready.

Start to finish: 15 minutes
Makes 4 servings

1   17-ounce package refrigerated cooked beef tips with gravy
½   cup onion-flavor beef broth
1   20-ounce package refrigerated mashed potatoes
2   tablespoons butter or margarine
⅛   teaspoon ground black pepper
4   thick slices white bread

1. In a large skillet, combine beef tips with gravy and broth. Cook and stir over medium heat until heated through.

2. Meanwhile, prepare mashed potatoes according to package directions, adding the butter and pepper.

3. To serve, place bread slices on four dinner plates. Divide mashed potatoes among bread slices. Ladle beef mixture over potatoes and bread. Serve immediately.

Per serving: 372 cal., 15 g total fat (6 g sat. fat), 64 mg chol., 1,174 mg sodium, 36 g carbo., 2 g fiber, 23 g pro.

Herbed Mayonnaise

Simply stirring chopped fresh herbs into mayonnaise makes for a delicous, quick sauce you can dollop over grilled steak, fish, or shrimp. Regular or low-fat mayonnaise works equally well—and you can stir in any herb or combination of herbs you like. Good choices include basil, dill, parsley, thyme, or tarragon.

Herbed Steaks with Horseradish

A horseradish, mustard, and herb mixture makes this steak dinner a cut above the ordinary.

Start to finish: 20 minutes
Makes 4 servings

2   12- to 14-ounce beef top loin steaks, cut 1 inch thick
    Salt and ground black pepper
2   tablespoons prepared horseradish
1   tablespoon Dijon-style mustard
2   teaspoons snipped fresh flat-leaf (Italian) parsley
1   teaspoon snipped fresh thyme
    Broiled cherry tomatoes (optional)
    Broiled sweet pepper strips (optional)
    Herbed mayonnaise (optional)

1. Preheat broiler; season steaks with salt and pepper. Place steaks on the unheated rack of a broiler pan. Broil 4 inches from heat for 7 minutes. Meanwhile, combine horseradish, mustard, parsley, and thyme.

2. Turn steaks. Broil 8 to 9 minutes more for medium (160°F). The last 1 minute of broiling, spread with horseradish mixture. If desired, serve with tomatoes, peppers, and herbed mayonnaise.

Per serving: 284 cal., 15 g total fat (6 g sat. fat), 84 mg chol., 351 mg sodium, 1 g carbo., 0 g fiber, 33 g pro.

Herbed Steaks with Horseradish

Sausage-Cavatelli Skillet

Cavatelli are bite-size pasta shells with ruffled edges. Here they're ideal for capturing every last drop of the zesty, saucy Italian sausage mixture.

Start to finish: 25 minutes
Makes 4 servings

- 8 ounces dried cavatelli (1¾ cups)
- 1 pound bulk Italian sausage or ground beef
- 1 medium green sweet pepper, chopped (optional)
- 1 20-ounce jar spaghetti sauce withmushrooms
- 1 cup shredded mozzarella cheese (4 ounces)

1. Cook cavatelli according to package directions. Drain well.

2. Meanwhile, in a large skillet, cook sausage or ground beef and sweet pepper (if desired) until meat is brown. Drain off fat. Stir spaghetti sauce into meat mixture; cook about 2 minutes or until heated through. Stir in the drained cavatelli. Sprinkle with cheese. Cover and cook about 2 minutes more or until cheese melts.

Per serving: 677 cal., 32 g total fat (13 g sat. fat), 93 mg chol., 1,469 mg sodium, 60 g carb., 4 g fiber, 32 g pro.

Cheese Choices

For cooks watching the clock, preshredded and grated cheeses can be real lifesavers. They not only eliminate work, but with the packages marked in cup amounts, it's easy to avoid unwanted leftovers. Check your supermarket's cheese section for what is available in your area. You should find both regular and finely shredded varieties for several types of cheese.

Saucy Strip Steak

Take one bite of tender, juicy steak and you'll agree there's nothing like this buttery blend of orange marmalade and rosemary to bring out the best in beef.

Prep: 15 minutes   **Grill:** 11 minutes
Makes 4 servings

- ⅔ cup orange marmalade
- 2 tablespoons butter or margarine
- 1 teaspoon snipped fresh rosemary or
- ¼ teaspoon dried rosemary, crushed
- 4 8-ounce boneless beef top loin steaks, cut 1 inch thick

1. In a small saucepan, combine marmalade, butter, and rosemary. Cook and stir over low heat until butter is melted and mixture is heated through. Set aside.

2. Sprinkle both sides of *each* steak with salt and ground black pepper. Place steaks on the rack of an uncovered grill directly over medium coals. Grill until desired doneness, turning once halfway through grilling and brushing with the marmalade mixture during the last 2 minutes of grilling. Allow 11 to 15 minutes for medium-rare doneness (145°F) or 14 to 18 minutes for medium doneness (160°F). Transfer steaks to a serving platter. Spoon any remaining marmalade mixture over steaks.

Per serving: 464 cal., 14 g total fat (7 g sat. fat), 123 mg chol., 357 mg sodium, 35 g carb., 0 g fiber, 49 g pro.

Towering Tostadas

Each family member can put together a do-it-yourself tostada with the help of taco-flavored shredded chicken and an assortment of veggies. For extra-creamy flavor, top each tostada with a spoonful of sour cream.

Start to finish: 15 minutes
Makes 4 to 6 servings

1	18-ounce tub taco sauce with shredded chicken*
8	to 12 6-inch tostada shells
1½	cups shredded peeled jicama, shredded carrot, packaged shredded broccoli (broccoli slaw mix), and/or canned black beans, rinsed and drained
⅔	cup shredded Colby and Monterey Jack cheese

1. In a medium saucepan, cook chicken mixture until heated through. Spoon chicken mixture onto tostada shells. Top with desired vegetables and cheese.

Per serving: 336 cal., 15 g total fat (6 g sat. fat), 74 mg chol., 1,197 mg sodium, 29 g carb., 3 g fiber, 17 g pro.

*Test Kitchen Tip: If you can't find this product, stir enough of your favorite bottled taco sauce into shredded cooked chicken to make it nicely saucy; heat through as directed.

Chicken and Biscuit Kabobs

Buttermilk biscuits bake right on the skewers with the chicken and squash for these classy kabobs. A drizzle of delicate honey butter adds a touch of richness.

Chicken and Biscuit Kabobs

Microwave-cooking the frozen chicken just a tad allows the skewers to be inserted easily. Instead of chicken, you can opt for thick slices of cooked smoked sausage. Thread slices onto the skewers with the biscuit dough and bake as directed.

Start to finish: 20 minutes
Oven: 400°F
Makes 4 servings

½ of a 13.5-ounce package (12) frozen cooked, breaded chicken breast chunks

1 4.5-ounce package (6) refrigerated buttermilk or country biscuits

1 medium zucchini or yellow summer squash,* cut into 3x¾-inch strips

⅓ cup butter, melted

3 tablespoons honey

1. Preheat oven to 400°F. Arrange chicken chunks in a single layer on a microwave-safe plate. Microwave, uncovered, on 100% power (high) for 1 minute (chicken will not be heated through).

2. Using kitchen scissors, snip each biscuit in half. On each of four wooden or metal skewers, alternately thread chicken pieces, biscuit halves, and zucchini strips, leaving a ¼-inch space between pieces. Place on ungreased baking sheet. Bake about 10 minutes or until biscuits are golden brown and chicken is heated through.

3. Meanwhile, whisk together melted butter and honey. Drizzle some of the butter mixture over kabobs. Pass remainder for dipping.

Per serving: 376 cal., 22 g total fat (9 g sat. fat), 57 mg chol., 649 mg sodium, 37 g carb., 1 g fiber, 10 g pro.

*Test Kitchen Tip: For extra color, use half of a medium zucchini and half of a medium yellow summer squash.

Chipotle Brisket Sandwich

Precooked sliced beef brisket makes it easy to prepare this stick-to-the-ribs barbecue sandwich whenever you like.

Start to finish: 15 minutes
Makes 6 servings

1 17-ounce package refrigerated cooked, seasoned, and sliced beef brisket with barbecue sauce

1 to 2 canned chipotle chile peppers in adobo sauce, chopped (see tip, page 58)

½ of a 16-ounce package shredded cabbage with carrot (coleslaw mix) (about 4 cups)

⅓ cup bottled coleslaw dressing

6 kaiser rolls, split and toasted

1. In a large saucepan, combine sliced beef and chopped chile peppers. Cook and stir about 5 minutes or until heated through.

2. Meanwhile, in a large bowl, combine shredded cabbage mix and coleslaw dressing.

3. To serve, spoon beef mixture onto roll bottoms. Top with coleslaw mixture. Top with roll tops.

Per serving: 414 cal., 18 g total fat (5 g sat. fat), 39 mg chol., 1,085 mg sodium, 47 g carb., 2 g fiber, 16 g pro.

Using Chipotles

Chipotle chile peppers are dried, smoked jalapeños. You'll find them canned in adobo sauce in the Mexican aisle of supermarkets or at Hispanic markets. Store the leftover chile peppers, covered, in the refrigerator for up to a week. They're terrific for adding pizzazz to pizzas, spicing up ground meat skillet dishes, stirring into taco or enchilada fillings, or topping scrambled eggs or omelets.

Bold-flavored shrimp seasoned with olive oil, jalapeño chile pepper, garlic, and tomatoes is perfect for **tossing with hot cooked linguine.** For extra flavor, sprinkle on Parmesan cheese.

Spicy Shrimp Pasta

Spicy Shrimp Pasta

Company coming? Stop at the store to pick up the ingredients you probably don't keep on hand: shrimp, pasta, chile peppers, and tomatoes. Grab some bottled minced garlic, oil, salt, and black pepper from your on-hand supply and start cooking.

Start to finish: 30 minutes
Makes 4 servings

- 12 ounces fresh or frozen large shrimp in shells
- 8 ounces dried linguine or fettuccine
- 2 tablespoons olive oil or cooking oil
- 1 or 2 fresh jalapeño chile peppers, finely chopped (see tip, page 58)
- 1 teaspoon bottled minced garlic
- ½ teaspoon salt
- ¼ teaspoon ground black pepper
- 2 cups cherry tomatoes, halved
  Finely shredded Parmesan cheese (optional)

1. Thaw shrimp, if frozen. Peel and devein shrimp. Rinse shrimp; pat dry with paper towels. Meanwhile, in a large saucepan, cook pasta according to package directions. Drain well. Return pasta to hot pan; cover to keep warm.

2. Meanwhile, in a large skillet, heat oil over medium-high heat. Add chile peppers, garlic, ½ teaspoon salt, and ¼ teaspoon ground black pepper; cook and stir for 1 minute. Add shrimp; cook about 3 minutes more or until shrimp are opaque. Stir in tomatoes; heat through.

3. Toss pasta with shrimp mixture. If desired, pass Parmesan cheese.

Per serving: 363 cal., 9 g total fat (1 g sat. fat), 97 mg chol., 396 mg sodium, 48 g carb., 3 g fiber, 21 g pro.

Lime-Poached Mahi Mahi

Basmati rice from India is an aromatic rice that's prized for its nutty flavor and sweet aroma. In this recipe, it is extraordinary with the margarita-accented fish.

Start to finish: 20 minutes
Makes 4 servings

- 4 6-ounce fresh or frozen mahi mahi or catfish fillets, ½ to ¾ inch thick
- 2 teaspoons seasoned pepper
- 1 tablespoon olive oil or cooking oil
- ⅓ cup frozen margarita mix concentrate, thawed
  Hot cooked basmati or long grain rice

1. Thaw fish, if frozen. Skin fish, if necessary. Rinse fish; pat dry with paper towels. Sprinkle both sides of each fish fillet with seasoned pepper. In a large nonstick skillet, heat oil over medium-high heat. Add fish fillets; cook for 2 to 4 minutes or until lightly browned, turning to brown evenly. Reduce heat to medium low. Carefully add the margarita mix concentrate to skillet. Cook, covered, for 6 to 8 minutes or until fish flakes easily when tested with a fork. Serve fish and cooking liquid with rice.

Per serving: 336 cal., 5 g total fat (1 g sat. fat), 124 mg chol., 150 mg sodium, 41 g carb., 0 g fiber, 34 g pro.

Garlic Hints

When every minute counts, bottled minced garlic cuts down on recipe preparation time. Look for it in the produce section of the supermarket. If you prefer to mince garlic cloves, substitute one clove garlic, minced, for each ½ teaspoon bottled minced garlic called for in a recipe.

Salmon Potato Cakes

Seafood seasoning, sometimes called Old Bay seasoning, originated in Maryland crab houses and typically is a mix of celery salt or seeds, bay leaves, and spices. It varies by brand and makes a delicious addition to fish dishes such as this one. Look for it in the herb and spice aisle of your supermarket.

Start to finish: 30 minutes
Makes 6 servings

1   **pound fresh or frozen salmon fillets**
3   **cups frozen shredded hash brown potatoes, thawed**
2   **eggs, slightly beaten**
1   **tablespoon seafood seasoning**
2   **tablespoons butter or margarine**

1. Thaw fish, if frozen. Rinse fish; pat dry with paper towels. In a covered large skillet, cook fish in a small amount of boiling water for 6 to 9 minutes or until fish flakes easily when tested with a fork. Remove skin, if present. Place fish in a large bowl and flake with a fork; cool slightly.

2. Add potatoes, eggs, and seafood seasoning to the fish; stir gently to combine. Shape fish mixture into six patties. In a 12-inch skillet, melt butter over medium heat. Add fish patties; cook about 8 minutes or until browned and heated through, turning once halfway through cooking.

Per serving: 235 cal., 9 g total fat (4 g sat. fat), 121 mg chol., 466 mg sodium, 19 g carb., 1 g fiber, 19 g pro.

Hearty Ham Stew

This sweet-and-saucy skillet meal works any time of year. When the weather's cold, it's ideal for chasing away the chills. In the summer, it's great fun to stir up over a campfire, camp stove, or grill.

Start to finish: 20 minutes
Makes 6 to 8 servings

2   **16-ounce cans pork and beans in tomato sauce**
1   **16-ounce package frozen mixed vegetables, thawed**
1   **8-ounce ham slice, cut into ½-inch cubes**
1   **tablespoon dried minced onion**
1   **cup broken corn chips (optional)**

1. In a 10-inch skillet, stir together pork and beans, mixed vegetables, ham, and dried minced onion. Cook over medium heat until bubbly, stirring occasionally. If desired, top individual servings with corn chips.

Per serving: 255 cal., 5 g total fat (2 g sat. fat), 32 mg chol., 1,189 mg sodium, 41 g carb., 10 g fiber, 17 g pro.

Take Your Choice

Frozen mixed vegetable combinations are an easy way to add veggies to a dish without a lot of preparation. For Hearty Ham Stew, you can choose from the classic medley of peas, corn, and beans or opt for a specialty combo such as zucchini, carrots, cauliflower, lima beans, and Italian beans. Just make sure to choose a product that does not include any sauce.

Hearty Ham Stew

Shrimp Quesadillas

Shrimp Quesadillas

Tired of beef tacos and burritos? Fill tortillas with hummus, shrimp, artichokes, and feta cheese for a flavorful 20-minute meal.

Start to finish: 20 minutes
Makes 4 servings

Nonstick cooking spray

4   **8-inch vegetable tortillas**

½   **of a 7-ounce carton garlic or spicy three-pepper hummus (⅓ cup)**

6   **ounces peeled, deveined cooked medium shrimp**

1   **6-ounce jar marinated artichoke hearts or ½ of a 16-ounce jar pickled mixed vegetables, drained and coarsely chopped**

1   **4-ounce package crumbled feta cheese**

1. Coat one side of each tortilla with cooking spray. Place tortillas, sprayed side down, on a work surface. Spread tortillas with hummus. Top half of each tortilla with shrimp, artichokes, and cheese. Fold tortillas in half, pressing gently.

2. Heat a large nonstick skillet or griddle over medium heat for 1 minute. Cook quesadillas, two at a time, for 4 to 6 minutes or until browned and heated through, turning once.

Per serving: 430 cal., 20 g total fat (7 g sat. fat), 108 mg chol., 1098 mg sodium, 42 g carbo., 4 g fiber, 21 g pro.

Curried Coconut Shrimp

Jasmine rice, a fragrant long-grain rice popular in Asian cooking, is aromatic, soft, and sticky when cooked.

Start to finish: 30 minutes
Makes 4 servings

1   **pound fresh or frozen large shrimp in shells, thawed (14 to 16 count)**

1   **cup uncooked jasmine rice**

1   **15¼-ounce can tropical fruit salad or pineapple chunks**

1   **teaspoon red curry paste**

1   **cup unsweetened coconut milk**

1. Thaw shrimp, if frozen. Prepare the rice according to package directions; set aside. Meanwhile, peel and devein the shrimp. Rinse and pat dry with paper towels; set aside. Drain liquid from fruit, reserving ½ cup. Set liquid and fruit aside.

2. In a large nonstick skillet, stir-fry the shrimp and curry paste over medium-high heat for 3 to 4 minutes or until shrimp turn opaque. Remove shrimp from skillet; set aside. Add coconut milk and reserved liquid from fruit to the skillet. Bring to boiling; reduce heat. Simmer, uncovered, for 5 to 7 minutes until mixture is slightly thickened and reduced to about 1 cup.

3. Divide hot cooked rice among four shallow bowls. Arrange shrimp on top of the rice and spoon the sauce over shrimp and rice. Top each serving with ¼ cup drained fruit.

Per serving: 463 cal., 17 g total fat (13 g sat. fat), 151 mg chol., 263 mg sodium, 55 g carbo., 2 g fiber, 24 g pro.

Pizza Margherita

Pizza Margherita

Although a pizza created in 1889 as a tribute to Queen Margherita of Savoy featured this combo of toppings, you'll need no royal baking staff to make this version. The up-to-date shortcut of starting with prepared dough gets this on the table fast.

Start to finish: 30 minutes
Oven: 450°F
Makes 4 servings

2	balls of prepared pizza dough or 1 13.8-ounce package refrigerated pizza crust*
1	tablespoon olive oil
1	teaspoon minced garlic (optional)
1	8-ounce can pizza sauce
12	ounces fresh mozzerella cheese, sliced
½	cup small fresh basil leaves

1. Preheat oven to 450°F. Lightly oil two 12-inch pizza pans or large baking sheets. Roll out pizza dough into two 12-inch rounds; place on prepared sheets. If using packaged refrigerated crust, divide dough in half and press each half into bottom of prepared pan. Bake for 10 minutes. Remove from oven and turn upside down on cooling racks. (If desired, cool completely and store in resealable plastic bags for up to one day.)

2. For pizza, place partially baked crusts on baking sheets or pizza pans. Combine olive oil and garlic, if using; brush atop crusts. Spoon half of the pizza sauce over each pizza; top with cheese. Sprinkle basil over pizzas. Bake for 10 to 12 minutes or until cheese is melted and slightly golden.

3. Place on large wooden cutting boards and cut with pizza cutter into narrow slices. Makes 8 main-dish or 16 appetizer servings

Per serving: 572 cal., 21 g total fat (10 g sat. fat), 30 mg chol., 1,110 mg sodium, 69 g carb., 3 g fiber, 25 g pro.

*Test Kitchen Tip: Some supermarkets and bakeries carry prepared pizza crust dough. You simply take it home and roll it out.

Cheesy Tortellini and Vegetables

Just about any frozen vegetable combination will work in this creamy pasta.

Start to finish: 20 minutes
Makes 4 servings

1	6-ounce package dried cheese-filled tortellini
1	16-ounce package loose-pack frozen broccoli, cauliflower, and carrots
1¼	cups milk
½	of a 1.8-ounce envelope white sauce mix (about 3 tablespoons)
6	ounces Havarti cheese with dill, cubed

1. Cook tortellini according to package directions, adding the frozen vegetables for the last 5 minutes of cooking. Drain well. Return tortellini mixture to hot pan; cover to keep warm.

2. Meanwhile, for sauce: In a small saucepan, whisk together milk and dry white sauce mix. Bring to boiling; reduce heat. Cook and stir for 1 minute. Remove from heat. Add cheese, stirring until melted. Pour sauce over tortellini mixture. Toss lightly.

Per serving: 453 cal., 24 g total fat (1 g sat. fat), 59 mg chol., 1,004 mg sodium, 38 g carb., 4 g fiber, 22 g pro.

Fresh Herbs

Snipping or shredding herbs for a recipe doesn't have to slow you down. To snip herbs quickly and easily, place the herbs in a glass measuring cup and use kitchen scissors to cut the leaves into tiny pieces. To shred herbs, tightly roll up the leaves into a cigar shape and cut across the roll into very thin slices.

Molasses-Glazed Pork Tenderloin

cooking
for company

Dinner for guests can be a cinch. Choose one of these enticing main dish recipes, add a couple of simple side dishes such as crusty rolls and buttered vegetables, and spend only half an hour in the kitchen— dinner will be ready when your company walks in the door.

Molasses-Glazed Pork Tenderloin

Consider old-fashioned corn bread as a charming dinner partner for this glazed pork with beans.

Start to finish: 30 minutes
Makes 4 servings

¼	cup finely chopped prosciutto or 2 slices bacon, coarsely chopped
2	9-ounce packages frozen cut green beans
½	cup chopped onion
¾	cup water
1	tablespoon olive oil
12	ounces pork tenderloin, cut into ½-inch-thick slices (11 to 12 slices)
½	cup orange juice
3	tablespoons molasses
1	teaspoon cornstarch
½	teaspoon salt
¼	teaspoon ground black pepper
	Steamed fresh spinach* (optional)

1. In a large skillet, cook prosciutto or bacon over medium heat until crisp; drain and set aside. In the same skillet, cook green beans and onion in the water according to bean package directions. Drain bean mixture; set aside.

2. In same skillet, heat oil over medium-high heat. Add pork tenderloin slices; cook for 4 to 5 minutes or just until barely pink in center, turning once halfway through cooking.

3. Meanwhile, in a small bowl, stir together orange juice, molasses, cornstarch, salt, and pepper. Add to meat in skillet. Cook and stir until thickened and bubbly. Cook and stir for 2 minutes more. Stir bean mixture into mixture in skillet; heat through.

4. If desired, serve with steamed spinach. Top individual servings with prosciutto or bacon.

Per serving: 258 cal., 7 g total fat (2 g sat. fat), 61 mg chol., 588 mg sodium, 27 g carb., 4 g fiber, 23 g pro.

***Test Kitchen Tip:** Purchase packaged prewashed fresh spinach and steam it for 3 to 5 minutes or just until tender.

Pork Chops with Raspberries

An unusual combination, perhaps, but once you—and your guests—taste this thick and bubbly sauce dotted with fresh berries, you'll want it again and again.

Start to finish: 25 minutes
Makes 4 servings

¾	cup reduced-sodium chicken broth
1	tablespoon white balsamic vinegar
1	tablespoon packed brown sugar
1½	teaspoons cornstarch
	Dash ground allspice
4	pork rib chops, cut ¾ inch thick (about 1½ pounds total)
½	teaspoon salt
¼	teaspoon ground black pepper
¼	teaspoon dried basil, crushed
1	tablespoon cooking oil
1	cup fresh raspberries

1. In a small bowl, stir together broth, balsamic vinegar, brown sugar, cornstarch, and allspice. Set aside.

2. Trim fat from chops. Sprinkle both sides of each chop with salt, pepper, and basil. In a 12-inch skillet, heat oil over medium heat. Add chops; cook for 8 to 12 minutes or until pork juices run clear (160°F). Transfer chops to a serving platter. Cover and keep warm. Drain fat from skillet.

3. Stir vinegar mixture. Add to skillet. Cook and stir over medium heat until slightly thickened and bubbly. Cook and stir for 2 minutes more. Gently stir in raspberries; heat through. To serve, spoon raspberry mixture over chops.

Per serving: 207 cal., 9 g total fat (2 g sat. fat), 53 mg chol., 444 mg sodium, 8 g carb., 2 g fiber, 22 g pro.

Balsamic Chicken and Vegetables

Balsamic vinegar, with its hallmark dark color, syrupy body, and slight sweetness, gives any recipe a wonderful out-of-the-ordinary touch.

Start to finish: 30 minutes
Makes 4 servings

¼	cup bottled Italian salad dressing
2	tablespoons balsamic vinegar
1	tablespoon honey
⅛	to ¼ teaspoon crushed red pepper
2	tablespoons olive oil
1	pound chicken breast tenderloins
10	ounces fresh asparagus, trimmed and cut into 2-inch pieces, or one 10-ounce package frozen cut asparagus, thawed and well drained
1	cup purchased shredded carrot
1	small tomato, seeded and chopped

1. In a small bowl, stir together salad dressing, balsamic vinegar, honey, and crushed red pepper. Set aside.

2. In a large skillet, heat oil over medium-high heat. Add chicken; cook for 5 to 6 minutes or until chicken is tender and no longer pink, turning once. Add half of the dressing mixture to the skillet; turn to coat chicken. Transfer chicken to a serving platter; cover and keep warm.

3. Add asparagus and carrot to skillet. Cook and stir for 3 to 4 minutes or until asparagus is crisp-tender; transfer to the serving platter.

4. Stir remaining dressing mixture; add to skillet. Cook and stir for 1 minute, scraping up browned bits from bottom of skillet. Drizzle dressing mixture over chicken and vegetables. Sprinkle with tomato.

Per serving: 269 cal., 12 g total fat (2 g sat. fat), 66 mg chol., 323 mg sodium, 12 g carb., 2 g fiber, 27 g pro.

Balsamic Chicken and Vegetables

This **colorful chicken dish** is delicious any time of year. In the spring and summer, make it with **fresh asparagus** when the tender stalks are at their peak. In fall and winter, rely on frozen cut asparagus.

Chicken with Creamy Mushrooms

Chicken with Creamy Mushrooms

Sliced mushrooms sizzled in butter add a woodsy accent to the marinated chicken. If you prefer, substitute plain chicken breast halves for the marinated ones.

Start to finish: 25 minutes
Makes 6 servings

3	tablespoons butter
1	pound packaged sliced fresh mushrooms (6 cups)
6	Italian-marinated skinless, boneless chicken breast halves (about 2 pounds total)
3	tablespoons rice vinegar or white wine vinegar
1½	cups whipping cream
3	tablespoons capers, rinsed and drained
¼	teaspoon freshly ground black pepper
	Steamed fresh vegetables (optional)

1. In a 12-inch skillet, heat 1 tablespoon of the butter over medium-high heat. Add mushrooms; cook about 5 minutes or until tender. Remove mushrooms from skillet.

2. Reduce heat to medium. Add the remaining 2 tablespoons butter and the breast halves to skillet. Cook for 8 to 12 minutes or until chicken is tender and no longer pink (170°F), turning once. Remove from skillet; cover and keep warm.

3. Remove skillet from heat; add vinegar, stirring to scrape up browned bits from bottom of skillet. Return skillet to heat. Stir in whipping cream, capers, and pepper. Bring to boiling; boil gently, uncovered, for 2 to 3 minutes or until sauce is slightly thickened. Return mushrooms to skillet; heat through. Serve chicken with mushroom mixture. If desired, serve with vegetables.

Per serving: 456 cal., 34 g total fat (19 g sat. fat), 183 mg chol., 967 mg sodium, 7 g carb., 1 g fiber, 33 g pro.

Rosemary Chicken with Vegetables

This garlic-laced rosemary sauce takes boneless chicken breasts from everyday to elegant fare in only 30 minutes.

Start to finish: 30 minutes
Makes 4 servings

4	skinless, boneless chicken breast halves (1¼ to 1½ pounds total)
½	teaspoon lemon-pepper seasoning
2	tablespoons olive oil
1	teaspoon bottled minced garlic
2	medium zucchini and/or yellow summer squash, cut into ¼-inch-thick slices
½	cup apple juice or apple cider
2	teaspoons snipped fresh rosemary or ½ teaspoon dried rosemary, crushed
4	ounces refrigerated linguine
2	tablespoons dry white wine
2	teaspoons cornstarch
12	cherry tomatoes, halved

1. Sprinkle chicken with lemon-pepper seasoning. In a large skillet, heat oil over medium heat. Add chicken; cook for 8 to 10 minutes or until chicken is tender and no longer pink (170°F), turning once halfway through cooking. Transfer chicken to a serving platter; cover and keep warm.

2. Add garlic to skillet; cook for 15 seconds. Add zucchini and/or summer squash, apple juice, and rosemary; bring to boiling. Reduce heat; cover and simmer for 2 minutes.

3. Meanwhile, cook pasta according to package directions; drain well. In a small bowl, combine wine and cornstarch; add to zucchini mixture in skillet. Cook and stir until thickened and bubbly; cook for 2 minutes more. Stir in tomato halves. Serve vegetables and pasta with chicken.

Per serving: 356 cal., 10 g total fat (2 g sat. fat), 103 mg chol., 235 mg sodium, 27 g carb., 2 g fiber, 38 g pro.

Pesto Penne with Roasted Chicken

Start to finish: 20 minutes
Makes 4 servings

8 ounces dried penne, mostacioli, or bow tie pasta (4 cups)
2 cups broccoli florets
1 2- to 2½ pound purchased roasted chicken
1 7-ounce container purchased basil
1 7-ounce jar roasted red sweet peppers, drained and cut into strips
¼ cup finely shredded Parmesan cheese
   Finely shredded Parmesan cheese (optional)
½ teaspoon coarsely ground black pepper

1. Cook pasta according to package directions, adding broccoli the last 2 minutes of cooking. Drain, reserving ½ cup of the pasta water. Return drained pasta and broccoli to saucepan.

2. Meanwhile, remove skin from chicken and discard. Remove chicken meat. Shred enough of the chicken meat to measure 2½ cups; set aside. Reserve any remaining chicken meat for another use.

3. In a small bowl, combine pesto and the reserved pasta water. Add chicken, roasted red sweet peppers, and pesto mixture to pasta in saucepan. Toss gently to coat. Heat through over medium heat. Add ¼ cup cheese to pasta mixture and toss to combine.

4. Divide the cooked pasta among four warm pasta bowls. If desired, sprinkle with additional Parmesan cheese. Top with black pepper.
Per serving: 672 cal., 35 g total fat (7 g sat. fat), 93 mg chol., 857 mg sodium, 53 g carbo., 3 g fiber, 37 g pro.

Chicken and Lemon-Broccoli Alfredo

Jazz up the flavor of purchased alfredo sauce with lemon peel and pepper for this chicken and mushroom skillet dinner.
Start to finish: 20 minutes
Makes 4 servings

4 small skinless, boneless chicken breast halves
   Salt and ground black pepper
8 ounces mushrooms, halved
1 tablespoon olive or cooking oil
1 lemon
3 cups fresh broccoli florets
1 10-ounce container refrigerated light Alfredo pasta sauce

1. Season chicken with salt and pepper. In a large skillet, cook chicken and mushrooms in hot oil for 4 minutes, turning chicken halfway through.

2. Meanwhile, shred 2 teaspoons lemon peel; set aside. Slice lemon. Add broccoli and lemon slices to skillet. Cook, covered, for 8 minutes or until chicken is done (170°F).

3. Place chicken and vegetables on plates. Add Alfredo sauce to skillet; heat through. Add lemon peel and pepper. Serve with chicken.
Per serving: 295 cal., 12 g total fat (5 g sat. fat), 91 mg chol., 705 mg sodium, 16 g carbo., 4 g fiber, 35 g pro.

Chicken and Lemon-Broccoli Alfredo

Chicken, Goat Cheese, and Greens

Just stop at the supermarket to pick up a ready-to-eat deli-roasted chicken and a few other ingredients and you'll have dinner ready in half an hour.

Prep: 15 minutes   **Bake:** 15 minutes
Oven: 350°F
Makes 4 servings

1½   pounds Swiss chard, beet greens, and/or mustard greens
 1   2- to 2½-pound purchased deli-roasted chicken
 3   tablespoons olive oil
 2   tablespoons lemon juice
 2   tablespoons snipped fresh dill, oregano, and/or sage
 ¼   teaspoon sea salt, kosher salt, or salt
 ¼   teaspoon cracked black pepper
 1   3- to 4-ounce log goat cheese (chèvre), sliced into rounds or coarsely crumbled

1. Preheat oven to 350°F. Trim and wash greens. Reserve two or three small leaves of the greens. Tear remaining greens; place in a 3-quart rectangular baking dish. Remove string from chicken; use string to tie the chicken legs together. Place chicken on greens in baking dish.

2. In a small bowl, combine oil and lemon juice; drizzle over chicken and greens in baking dish. Sprinkle 1 tablespoon of the dill over chicken and greens. Sprinkle the salt and ⅛ teaspoon of the pepper over just the greens in baking dish.

3. Loosely cover baking dish with foil. Bake for 15 to 20 minutes or until greens are tender. Meanwhile, sprinkle cheese with the remaining 1 tablespoon dill and ⅛ teaspoon pepper.

4. Transfer chicken to a serving platter. Place some of the goat cheese on top of chicken. Add reserved greens. Toss cooked greens in dish to evenly coat with cooking liquid. Serve cooked greens and remaining cheese with chicken.

Per serving: 542 cal., 36 g total fat (10 g sat. fat), 143 mg chol., 620 mg sodium, 7 g carb., 3 g fiber, 48 g pro.

Fettuccine Verona

Named for the city of Romeo and Juliet, this chicken dish is studded with tomatoes and zucchini.

Start to finish: 20 minutes
Makes 4 servings

 1   9-ounce package refrigerated fettuccine
 ¼   of a 7-ounce jar oil-packed dried tomato strips or pieces (¼ cup)
 1   large zucchini or yellow summer squash, halved lengthwise and sliced
 8   ounces packaged skinless, boneless chicken breast strips (stir-fry strips)
 2   tablespoons olive oil
 ½   cup finely shredded Parmesan cheese
      Freshly ground black pepper

1. Using kitchen scissors, cut fettuccine strands in half. Cook fettuccine according to package directions. Drain well. Return fettuccine to hot pan; cover to keep warm.

2. Meanwhile, drain dried tomatoes, reserving 2 tablespoons of the oil. Set drained tomatoes aside. In a large skillet, heat 1 tablespoon of the reserved oil over medium-high heat. Add zucchini; cook and stir for 2 to 3 minutes or until crisp-tender. Remove from skillet. Add the remaining 1 tablespoon reserved oil to skillet. Add chicken; cook and stir 2 to 3 minutes or until no longer pink.

3. Add chicken, zucchini, drained tomatoes, and olive oil to cooked fettuccine; toss gently to combine. Sprinkle individual servings with cheese. Season to taste with pepper.

Per serving: 384 cal., 14 g total fat (4 g sat. fat), 93 mg chol., 356 mg sodium, 37 g carb., 4 g fiber, 28 g pro.

Chicken, Goat Cheese, and Greens

A drizzle of the **peanut butter** dressing makes the perfect partner for these stacks built from napa cabbage, **deli-roasted chicken,** green grapes, chunks of apple, and **pineapple spears.**

Stack-It-Up Chicken Salad

Stack-It-Up Chicken Salad

If time is short, skip stacking the salad ingredients and toss them in a large bowl with the dressing.
Start to finish: 30 minutes
Makes 4 servings

1   peeled, cored fresh pineapple
1   2- to 2¼-pound purchased deli-roasted chicken
½   of a head napa cabbage, cut crosswise into 1-inch pieces
1   cup seedless green grapes, halved
1   Granny Smith apple, cut into chunks
½   cup bottled ginger-sesame stir-fry sauce
¼   cup creamy peanut butter
¼   teaspoon crushed red pepper

1. Cut pineapple lengthwise into ½-inch-wide spears. Remove skin from chicken and discard. Remove meat from bones; discard bones. Cut chicken into bite-size pieces. On each of four dinner plates, build a stack using the cabbage, chicken, grapes, apple chunks, and pineapple.

2. For dressing: In a small bowl, whisk together stir-fry sauce, peanut butter, and crushed red pepper. If necessary, whisk in water, 1 teaspoon at a time, until dressing reaches drizzling consistency. Drizzle dressing over arranged salads.

Per serving: 529 cal., 19 g total fat (5 g sat. fat), 123 mg chol., 998 mg sodium, 44 g carb., 5 g fiber, 45 g pro.

Turkey Piccata

The tasty juices left in the skillet after cooking the turkey jump-start the snappy pan sauce.
Start to finish: 30 minutes
Makes 4 servings

6   ounces dried fettuccine or linguine
¼   cup all-purpose flour
½   teaspoon lemon-pepper seasoning
2   turkey breast tenderloins (about 1 pound total)
2   tablespoons olive oil or cooking oil
⅓   cup dry white wine
2   tablespoons lemon juice
2   tablespoons water
½   teaspoon instant chicken bouillon granules
1   tablespoon capers, rinsed and drained (optional)
2   tablespoons snipped fresh parsley
    Lemon wedges (optional)
    Fresh parsley sprigs (optional)

1. Cook pasta according to package directions. Drain well. Return pasta to hot pan; cover to keep warm. Meanwhile, in a small bowl, stir together flour and lemon-pepper seasoning; set aside.

2. Cut each turkey tenderloin crosswise into ½-inch-thick slices. Dip turkey slices in flour mixture to coat.

3. In a large skillet, heat oil over medium-high heat. Add turkey; cook for 6 to 10 minutes or until light golden brown and no longer pink (170°F), turning once halfway through cooking. Remove turkey from skillet; cover and keep warm.

4. For sauce: Add wine, lemon juice, the water, and bouillon granules to skillet, scraping up browned bits from bottom of skillet. If desired, stir in capers. Bring to boiling; reduce heat. Simmer, uncovered, for 2 minutes. Remove from heat; stir in snipped parsley.

5. To serve, divide pasta among four dinner plates. Top pasta with turkey slices. Spoon sauce over all. If desired, serve with lemon wedges and garnish with parsley sprigs.

Per serving: 377 cal., 9 g total fat (2 g sat. fat), 68 mg chol., 301 mg sodium, 36 g carb., 1 g fiber, 33 g pro.

Turkey Marsala with Mushrooms

This takeoff of a classic veal dish features slices of turkey breast tenderloin.

Start to finish: 30 minutes
Makes 4 servings

- 1 turkey breast tenderloin (about 8 ounces)
- 2 tablespoons all-purpose flour
- ¾ teaspoon salt
- ¼ teaspoon ground black pepper
- 4 teaspoons olive oil or cooking oil
- 12 ounces packaged sliced fresh mushrooms (4½ cups)
- ½ cup chopped onion
- ¼ teaspoon dried thyme, crushed
- ½ cup chicken broth
- ⅓ cup dry Marsala wine or dry sherry
- 1 teaspoon cornstarch

1. Cut turkey tenderloin crosswise into ¼-inch-thick slices. In a shallow dish, combine flour, ½ teaspoon of the salt, and the pepper. Dip turkey slices into flour mixture to coat.

2. In a large skillet, cook turkey slices, half at a time, in hot oil for 2 to 4 minutes or until golden brown and no longer pink, turning once halfway through cooking. (Add more oil as necessary during cooking.) Remove turkey from skillet.

3. Add mushrooms, onion, thyme, and the remaining ¼ teaspoon salt to the skillet. Cook and stir for 4 to 5 minutes or until mushrooms and onion are tender. In a small bowl, stir together broth, wine, and cornstarch; carefully stir into mixture in skillet. Cook and stir until thickened and bubbly. Cook and stir for 2 minutes more.

4. Return turkey slices to skillet; heat through.

Per serving: 235 cal., 8 g total fat (1 g sat. fat), 68 mg chol., 621 mg sodium, 8 g carb., 1 g fiber, 30 g pro.

Chipotle-Sauced Crab Cakes

This recipe is a restaurant favorite, but our version is super-simple to whip up at home. To tame the spiciness of the Chipotle Sauce, remove the seeds from the pepper before you add it to the rest of the ingredients.

Start to finish: 30 minutes
Makes 4 servings

- 1 egg, slightly beaten
- ¾ cup soft bread crumbs (1 slice)
- 2 tablespoons sliced green onion
- 2 tablespoons mayonnaise or salad dressing
- 1 tablespoon milk
- ½ teaspoon lemon-pepper seasoning
- 2 6½-ounce cans crabmeat, drained, flaked, and cartilage removed
- Nonstick cooking spray
- 4 cups torn mixed salad greens
- Chipotle Sauce

1. In a large bowl, stir together egg, bread crumbs, green onion, mayonnaise, milk, and lemon-pepper seasoning. Add crabmeat; mix well. Shape into eight 2½-inch patties.

2. Lightly coat an unheated large nonstick skillet with nonstick cooking spray. Preheat over medium heat. Add crab patties. Cook for 6 to 8 minutes or until browned, turning once. Serve crab patties with greens and Chipotle Sauce.

Chipotle Sauce: In a small bowl, stir together ⅓ cup mayonnaise or salad dressing; ¼ cup dairy sour cream; 2 tablespoons milk; 2 teaspoons snipped fresh cilantro; 1 canned chipotle chile pepper in adobo sauce, drained and finely chopped (see tip, page 58); and dash salt.

Per serving: 359 cal., 26 g total fat (6 g sat. fat), 150 mg chol., 712 mg sodium, 8 g carb., 1 g fiber, 23 g pro.

Chipotle-Sauced Crab Cakes

A smoky chipotle **chile pepper** gives the creamy no-cook sauce gusto that complements the **subtly seasoned** crab cakes and greens.

Orange marmalade adds **sweetness,** Dijon-style mustard tang, and five-spice powder a hint of intrigue to **fork-tender salmon** fillets served with crisp-tender asparagus spears.

Citrus-Glazed Salmon

Citrus-Glazed Salmon

To save even more time, look for bottled grated ginger in your supermarket's produce section.

Prep: 15 minutes
Bake: 4 minutes per ½-inch thickness
Oven: 450°F
Makes 8 servings

1   **2-pound fresh or frozen salmon fillet, skin
    removed**
    Salt
    Ground black pepper
¾   **cup orange marmalade**
2   **green onions, sliced**
2   **teaspoons dry white wine**
1   **teaspoon grated fresh ginger**
1   **teaspoon Dijon-style mustard**
½   **teaspoon bottled minced garlic**
¼   **teaspoon cayenne pepper**
⅛   **teaspoon five-spice powder**
3   **tablespoons sliced almonds, toasted**
    Steamed fresh asparagus spears*
    (optional)

1. Thaw fish, if frozen. Preheat oven to 450°F. Rinse fish; pat dry with paper towels. Measure the thickest portion of the fish fillet. Sprinkle with salt and pepper. Place in shallow baking pan; set aside.

2. In a small bowl, stir together marmalade, green onions, wine, ginger, mustard, garlic, cayenne pepper, and five-spice powder. Spoon over fish.

3. Bake for 4 to 6 minutes per ½-inch thickness or until fish flakes easily when tested with a fork. If desired, serve fish with asparagus. Sprinkle individual servings with almonds.

Per serving: 227 cal., 6 g total fat (1 g sat. fat), 59 mg chol., 170 mg sodium, 21 g carb., 1 g fiber, 24 g pro.

*Test Kitchen Tip: To steam fresh asparagus, snap off and discard woody bases from spears. Steam spears for 4 to 6 minutes or until tender.

Broiled Halibut with Dijon Cream

Your guests will "ooh" and "ahh" over this special dish. If there are no halibut steaks at the fish counter, feel free to try sea bass or cod instead.

Start to finish: 15 minutes
Makes 4 servings

4   **fresh or frozen halibut steaks, cut 1 inch
    thick (1 to 1½ pounds total)**
1   **teaspoon Greek-style seasoning blend**
¼   **teaspoon coarsely ground black pepper**
¼   **cup dairy sour cream**
¼   **cup creamy Dijon-style mustard blend**
1   **tablespoon milk**
½   **teaspoon dried oregano, crushed**

1. Preheat broiler. Thaw fish, if frozen. Rinse fish; pat dry with paper towels. Grease the unheated rack of a broiler pan; place fish on rack. Sprinkle fish with Greek-style seasoning blend and pepper.

2. Broil 4 inches from the heat for 8 to 12 minutes or until fish flakes easily when tested with a fork, turning once halfway through broiling. Invert fish onto a serving platter.

3. Meanwhile, for sauce: In a small bowl, combine sour cream, mustard blend, milk, and oregano. Serve sauce over fish.

Per serving: 168 cal., 5 g total fat (2 g sat. fat), 42 mg chol., 300 mg sodium, 4 g carb., 0 g fiber, 24 g pro.

Pick a Blend

Herb and spice blends save you the time of measuring a number of seasonings. The Greek-style seasoning used in Broiled Halibut with Dijon Cream is typically a mix of lemon, garlic, and oregano plus other flavorings. Because each brand is different, try several until you find the one you like best. Other blends include Cajun seasoning, Italian seasoning, fines herbes, herbes de Provence, lemon-pepper seasoning, and Jamaican jerk seasoning.

Salmon En Papillote

En Papillote means "in a paper casing" in French. It refers to a method of oven-steaming food—usually fish and herbs or vegetables—in a package of parchment paper. It's a light and healthy way to cook.

Salmon en Papillote

Start to finish: 20 minutes   **Oven:** 375°F
Makes 4 servings

    4   12-inch squares parchment paper
    4   skinless salmon fillets (about 1¼ pounds
         total)
    1   tablespoon olive oil
    ⅛   teaspoon ground black pepper
    1   tablespoon snipped fresh mint
    1   tablespoon snipped fresh dill
    4   thin slices lemon, halved or quartered
    1   tablespoon drained capers
         Dill sprigs and/or lemon wedges (optional)

1. Preheat oven to 375°F. Place one fish portion in the middle of each parchment square. Drizzle with olive oil and sprinkle with pepper. Top each mint, dill, lemon pieces, and capers. Bring up two opposite sides of parchment and fold several times over fish. Fold remaining ends of parchment and tuck under. Place fish packets in a shallow baking pan.

2. Bake for 13 to 15 minutes or until fish flakes easily when tested with a fork, carefully opening one packet to test doneness. Carefully open each packet to serve. If desired, garnish with fresh dill sprigs and/or lemon wedges.

Per serving: 292 cal., 19 g total fat (4 g sat. fat), 84 mg chol., 148 mg sodium, 0.9 g carbo., 0.4 g fiber, 28 g pro.

Tilapia with Ginger-Marinated Cucumbers

A brief soak in vinegar, sugar, ginger, and salt turns the cucumbers into an Asian-style pickle to serve with fish.
Start to finish: 20 minutes
Makes 4 servings

    4   4-ounce fresh or frozen tilapia fillets,
         ½ to ¾ inch thick
    ½   cup cider vinegar
    ¼   cup packed brown sugar
    2   teaspoons grated fresh ginger
    ½   teaspoon salt
  3½   cups sliced cucumber (2 medium)
    2   tablespoons coarsely chopped fresh mint
         Nonstick cooking spray
    1   6-ounce container plain yogurt
    1   teaspoon packed brown sugar
         Lemon peel and lemon wedges (optional)
         Cracked peppercorns (optional)

1. Thaw fish, if frozen. Preheat broiler. In a medium bowl, combine vinegar, ¼ cup brown sugar, ginger, and salt; stir until sugar dissolves. Remove ¼ cup of the mixture. Add cucumber and 1 tablespoon mint to remaining mixture in bowl; toss to coat and set aside.

2. Lightly coat the rack of an unheated broiler pan with cooking spray. Place fish on rack. Brush the ¼ cup vinegar mixture over the fish. Broil 4 inches from the heat for 4 to 6 minutes or until fish begins to flake when tested with a fork.

3. Meanwhile, in another small bowl, combine yogurt, the remaining 1 tablespoon mint, and the 1 teaspoon brown sugar.

4. Using a slotted spoon, place cucumbers on 4 plates. Top with fish and yogurt mixture. If desired, garnish with lemon peel, lemon wedges, and cracked peppercorns.

Per serving: 210 cal., 3 g total fat (1 g sat. fat), 59 mg chol., 388 mg sodium, 23 g carbo., 0 g fiber, 26 g pro.

Pan-Seared Tilapia with Almond Browned Butter

Pan-searing gives the fish a golden crust and locks in flavor and natural juices. If you try to turn the fish fillets and there's some resistance, cook them a little longer, and try again.

Start to finish: 25 minutes
Makes 4 servings

4	4- to 5-ounce skinless fresh or frozen tilapia fillets or other white fish
3	cups fresh pea pods, trimmed
1	teaspoon all-purpose flour
1	tablespoon olive oil
2	tablespoons butter
¼	cup coarsely chopped almonds
1	tablespoon snipped fresh parsley

1. Thaw fish, if frozen. Rinse fish; pat dry with paper towels. Set aside. In a large saucepan, bring a large amount of lightly salted water to boiling. Add pea pods; cook 2 minutes. Drain; set aside.

2. Meanwhile, sprinkle *one side* of *each* fish fillet with salt and ground black pepper; sprinkle with the flour. Preheat a large skillet over medium-high heat. When skillet is hot (a drop of water should sizzle or roll), remove from heat; immediately add oil, tilting skillet to coat with oil. Return skillet to heat; add fish, floured sides up (if necessary, cook fish half at a time). Cook fish for 4 to 5 minutes or until it is easy to move with a spatula. Gently turn fish; cook for 2 to 3 minutes more or until fish flakes easily when tested with a fork. Arrange pea pods on a serving platter; arrange fish on top of pea pods.

3. Reduce heat to medium. Add butter to the skillet. When butter begins to melt, stir in almonds. Cook for 30 to 60 seconds or until nuts are lightly toasted (do not let butter burn). Spoon butter mixture over fish. Sprinkle with parsley.

Per serving: 266 cal., 15 g total fat (5 g sat. fat), 71 mg chol., 210 mg sodium, 7 g carb., 3 g fiber, 24 g pro.

Spring Salmon Chowder

To quick-thaw the corn, place it in a colander and rinse it with cold running water.

Start to finish: 25 minutes
Makes 6 servings

2	14-ounce cans vegetable broth
6	tiny new potatoes, quartered
½	cup loose-pack frozen whole kernel corn, thawed
½	teaspoon dried thyme, crushed
12	ounces fresh or frozen skinless, boneless salmon, cut into 1-inch chunks
1	cup packed fresh baby spinach leaves
¼	cup sliced green onions
	Salt
	Ground black pepper

1. In a large saucepan, bring vegetable broth to boiling. Add quartered potatoes; cover and cook about 5 minutes or until potatoes are tender but not cooked through. Add corn and thyme. Return to boiling; reduce heat. Cover and cook about 4 minutes or until the vegetables are tender. Reduce the heat.

2. Carefully add salmon chunks to mixture in saucepan. Simmer, uncovered, for 3 to 5 minutes or until salmon flakes easily when tested with a fork. Stir in spinach and green onions; cook about 1 minute or until spinach begins to wilt. Season to taste with salt and pepper.

Per serving: 149 cal., 6 g total fat (1 g sat. fat), 33 mg chol., 607 mg sodium, 10 g carb., 1 g fiber, 13 g pro.

Spring Salmon Chowder

This broth-based chowder is brimming with **spring flavors.** Baby spinach and green onions nicely accent the **new potatoes and salmon.**

Scallops and Spinach with Parmesan Sauce

The pairing of a hot mixture with cool greens sets this dish apart. You'll love the way the greens wilt pleasantly as they meld with the luscious, creamy scallop mixture.

Start to finish: 25 minutes
Makes 4 servings

- 1   pound fresh or frozen large sea scallops
- 6   cups purchased torn Italian-blend salad greens or prewashed baby spinach
- 4   small red and/or yellow tomatoes, cut into chunks
- 3   tablespoons butter or margarine
- 1   teaspoon bottled minced garlic
- ¼   teaspoon cayenne pepper
- 1   tablespoon all-purpose flour
- ¾   cup half-and-half or light cream
- ⅓   cup grated Parmesan cheese

1. Thaw scallops, if frozen. Rinse scallops; pat dry with paper towels.

2. Preheat broiler. Divide greens among four dinner plates. Arrange tomato chunks on top of greens; set aside.

3. Arrange scallops on unheated rack of a broiler pan; set aside. In small saucepan, melt butter over medium heat; stir in garlic and cayenne pepper. Remove from heat. Brush half of the butter mixture on scallops. Broil scallops 4 inches from heat about 8 minutes or until opaque, turning once halfway through broiling. (If desired for easier turning, thread scallops on metal skewers before broiling.)

4. Meanwhile, return saucepan to heat; stir flour into remaining butter mixture in saucepan. Add half-and-half and Parmesan cheese; cook and stir until thickened and bubbly. Cook and stir for 1 minute more.

5. Arrange broiled scallops on top of tomato on plates; drizzle with Parmesan cheese mixture.
Per serving: 310 cal., 18 g total fat (11 g sat. fat), 85 mg chol., 464 mg sodium, 12 g carb., 2 g fiber, 26 g pro.

Garlicky Steak and Asparagus

A steak, a handful of asparagus, and a few minutes on an indoor grill are all you need to put together this savory feast for you and someone special.

Prep: 15 minutes
Grill: 3 minutes (covered indoor grill) or 6 minutes (uncovered indoor grill)
Makes 2 servings

- 1   or 2 large cloves garlic, coarsely chopped
- ½   teaspoon cracked or coarsely ground black pepper
- ¼   teaspoon salt
- 1   12- to 14-ounce boneless beef top loin (strip) steak, cut about ¾ inch thick
- 8   to 10 thin fresh asparagus spears, trimmed (6 ounces)
- 2   teaspoons garlic-flavored olive oil or olive oil
- ½   cup beef broth
- 1   tablespoon dry white wine
- ¼   teaspoon Dijon-style mustard

1. In a small bowl, combine garlic, pepper, and salt. Sprinkle garlic mixture evenly over steak; press in with your fingers. Place the asparagus in a shallow dish; drizzle with the oil.

2. For sauce: In a medium skillet, stir together beef broth and wine. Cook over high heat for 4 to 5 minutes or until reduced to ¼ cup. Whisk in mustard; keep warm.

3. Preheat an indoor electric grill on high setting, if available. Place the steak on the grill rack. If using a covered grill, close lid. Grill until steak is desired doneness. (For a covered indoor grill, allow 3 to 4 minutes for medium-rare doneness [145°F] or 5 to 7 minutes for medium doneness [160°F]. For an uncovered grill, allow 6 to 8 minutes for medium-rare doneness [145°F] or 8 to 10 minutes for medium doneness [160°F], turning steak once.) If space allows, add the asparagus to covered grill for the last 2 to 3 minutes or to uncovered grill the last 4 to 5 minutes of grilling. Cook asparagus just until crisp-tender.*

4. Spoon sauce onto serving plate. Cut steak in half crosswise. Serve steak halves on top of sauce. Serve with asparagus.

Per serving: 458 cal., 32 g total fat (11 g sat. fat), 110 mg chol., 549 mg sodium, 3 g carb., 1 g fiber, 37 g pro.

Broiler Directions: Preheat broiler. Place steak on the unheated rack of a broiler pan. Broil steak 3 to 4 inches from the heat until desired doneness, turning once and adding the asparagus spears to the rack of the broiler pan for the last 2 minutes of broiling. Allow 8 to 10 minutes for medium-rare doneness (145°F) or 10 to 12 minutes for medium doneness (160°F).

*Test Kitchen Tip: The asparagus cooking time will vary with the size of the asparagus spears. Also, if there is no room on the grill, the asparagus can be grilled after the steak; grill for 2 to 5 minutes or just until crisp-tender.

Garlicky Steak and Asparagus

Beef and Broccoli with Plum Sauce

If you can't find plums, substitute 1 cup frozen unsweetened peach slices, thawed and cut up.
Start to finish: 30 minutes
Makes 4 servings

12	ounces beef top round steak
¾	cup water
½	cup bottled plum sauce
2	tablespoons reduced-sodium soy sauce
1	tablespoon cornstarch
1	teaspoon grated fresh ginger
1	tablespoon cooking oil
1	cup broccoli florets
1	small onion, cut into 1-inch pieces
1	teaspoon bottled minced garlic
3	cups lightly packed, coarsely chopped bok choy
2	medium plums, pitted and cut into thin wedges
	Hot cooked fine egg noodles or rice

1. Trim fat from steak. Thinly slice steak across the grain into bite-size strips. Set aside. For sauce: In a small bowl, stir together the water, plum sauce, soy sauce, cornstarch, and ginger. Set aside.

2. In a nonstick wok or large skillet, heat oil over medium-high heat. (Add more oil as necessary during cooking.) Add broccoli, onion, and garlic; stir-fry for 3 minutes. Remove broccoli mixture from wok. Add beef to hot wok. Cook and stir for 2 to 3 minutes or until brown. Push beef from center of wok. Stir sauce. Add sauce to center of wok. Cook and stir until thickened and bubbly.

3. Return broccoli mixture to wok. Add bok choy and plums. Stir all ingredients together to coat with sauce. Cover and cook about 2 minutes more or until heated through. Serve over noodles or rice.

Per serving: 413 cal., 10 g total fat (3 g sat. fat), 74 mg chol., 533 mg sodium, 54 g carb., 4 g fiber, 26 g pro.

Country French Ribeyes

Elevate yourself to the rank of master griller with these juicy, lavender-infused ribeyes. If you have time to plan ahead, you can boost the lavender flavor by applying the rub a few hours in advance and refrigerating the steaks.
Prep: 10 minutes   **Grill:** 16 minutes
Makes 4 servings

5	green onions
2	teaspoons dried lavender, crushed
2	teaspoons dried thyme, crushed
1	teaspoon coarsely ground black pepper
½	teaspoon coarse salt
4	6- to 8-ounce boneless beef ribeye steaks, cut 1 to 1¼ inches thick
1	tablespoon olive oil
4	to 8 plum tomatoes

1. Mince *one* of the green onions; set remaining green onions aside. In a small bowl, combine minced green onion, lavender, thyme, pepper, and coarse salt. Sprinkle green onion mixture evenly over steaks; rub in with your fingers. Brush steaks with half of the olive oil. Brush plum tomatoes and the remaining green onions with the remaining olive oil.

2. Place steaks on the lightly oiled rack of an uncovered grill directly over medium-high coals. Grill for 8 minutes. Place tomatoes and green onions alongside steaks on grill. Turn steaks; grill for 8 to 10 minutes more or until desired doneness (145°F for medium-rare doneness; 160°F for medium doneness). Grill tomatoes and onions for 8 to 10 minutes or until slightly charred, turning several times.

Per serving: 326 cal., 17 g total fat (6 g sat. fat), 99 mg chol., 340 mg sodium, 5 g carb., 2 g fiber, 36 g pro.

Country French Ribeyes

Wine-Balsamic Glazed Steak

For variety and a rich earthiness, try a mixture of button, crimini, shiitake, and portobello mushrooms. The alcohol in the red wine is cooked off leaving just the delightful flavor.

Start to finish: 30 minutes
Makes 4 servings

2   teaspoons cooking oil
1   pound boneless beef top loin or top sirloin steak, cut ½ to ¾ inch thick
3   cloves garlic, minced
⅛   teaspoon crushed red pepper
¾   cup dry red wine
2   cups sliced fresh mushrooms
3   tablespoons balsamic vinegar
2   tablespoons soy sauce
4   teaspoons honey
2   tablespoons butter

1. In a large skillet, heat oil over medium-high heat until very hot. Add steak. (Do not add liquid and do not cover the skillet.) Reduce heat to medium and cook for 10 to 13 minutes or to desired doneness, turning meat occasionally. If meat browns too quickly, reduce heat to medium-low. Transfer meat to platter; keep warm.

2. Add garlic and red pepper to skillet; cook for 10 seconds. Remove skillet from heat. Carefully add wine. Return to heat. Boil, uncovered, about 5 minutes or until most of the liquid is evaporated. Add mushrooms, vinegar, soy sauce, and honey; return to simmer. Cook and stir about 4 minutes or until mushrooms are tender. Stir in butter until melted. Spoon over steak.

Per serving: 377 cal., 21 g total fat (9 g sat. fat), 82 mg chol., 588 mg sodium, 12 g carbo., 0 g fiber, 27 g pro.

Steak with Sautéed Onions

Start to finish: 25 minutes
Makes 6 servings

6   4-ounce beef tenderloin steaks, cut 1 inch thick
¼   teaspoon salt
¼   teaspoon ground black pepper
2   tablespoons butter or margarine
1   small red onion, cut into 6 wedges
2   cloves garlic, minced
1   teaspoon dried basil, crushed
½   teaspoon dried oregano, crushed
2   tablespoons whipping cream
6   tablespoons onion marmalade or orange marmalade
    Snipped fresh parsley (optional)

1. Sprinkle steaks with salt and pepper. In a large skillet, melt butter over medium heat. Add onion and garlic. Cook, stirring frequently, for 6 to 8 minutes or until onion is tender but not brown. Remove onion from skillet; set aside.

2. Add steaks to the hot skillet. Cook steaks to desired doneness, turning occasionally. Allow 10 to 13 minutes for medium rare (145°F) to medium (160°F). After turning, sprinkle steaks with basil and oregano the last 2 minutes of cooking.

3. Remove steaks from skillet; place on plates and keep warm. Return onions to skillet. Heat onions through. Remove skillet from heat. Stir in whipping cream. Spoon cream over steaks. Top each steak with 1 tablespoon of the marmalade. Divide cooked onions evenly among the steaks. If desired, sprinkle with parsley.

Per serving: 271 cal., 13 g total fat (4 g sat. fat), 63 mg chol., 110 mg sodium, 14 g carbo., 0 g fiber, 24 g pro.

Steak with Sautéed Onions

Sautéed sweet red onion wedges cooked with
a whisper of cream and onion marmalade make an
elegant topping for **juicy pan-broiled steaks.**

Steak with Pear Brandy-Black Pepper Sauce

The **pear brandy** and caramel-like flavor of dried pears transform a simple sauce into an extraordinary topper for **beef tenderloin steaks**. Serve the captivating combination with your favorite potatoes.

Steak with Pear Brandy-Black Pepper Sauce

You'll find pear brandy at fine wine and liquor shops. In a pinch, pear nectar works instead of the brandy.
Start to finish: 30 minutes
Makes 4 servings

½ cup snipped dried pears
⅓ cup pear brandy or pear nectar
4 teaspoons all-purpose flour
1 teaspoon cracked black pepper
½ teaspoon salt
4 beef tenderloin or top loin steaks, cut 1 inch thick (1 to 1½ pounds total)
3 tablespoons butter
¼ cup finely chopped shallots or green onions
¼ cup reduced-sodium beef broth

1. In a small bowl, stir together dried pears and pear brandy; cover and let stand for 15 minutes.

2. Meanwhile, in a shallow dish, stir together flour, pepper, and salt. Dip steaks in flour mixture, turning to coat. In large skillet, melt 2 tablespoons of the butter over medium heat. Add steaks; cook until desired doneness, turning once halfway through cooking. For beef tenderloin steaks, allow 10 to 13 minutes for medium-rare doneness (145°F) to medium doneness (160°F). For beef top loin steaks, allow 12 to 15 minutes for medium-rare doneness (145°F) to medium doneness (160°F). Transfer steaks to a serving platter, reserving the drippings in the skillet. Cover and keep warm.

3. For sauce: In same skillet, cook shallots in the reserved drippings over medium heat for 1 minute. Remove from heat. Let stand for 1 minute. Stir in pear mixture and broth. Bring to boiling. Boil gently, uncovered, about 3 minutes or until slightly thickened, stirring occasionally. Whisk in remaining 1 tablespoon butter. Spoon sauce over steaks.

Per serving: 322 cal., 17 g total fat (8 g sat. fat), 81 mg chol., 465 mg sodium, 6 g carb., 0 g fiber, 24 g pro.

Veal with Orange Sauce

Fresh ginger enhances the sauce's orange flavor.
Start to finish: 25 minutes
Makes 4 servings

2 medium oranges
12 ounces veal scaloppine or boneless veal leg round steak or sirloin steak, cut ¼ inch thick
¼ teaspoon salt
¼ teaspoon ground black pepper
2 teaspoons olive oil
⅓ cup sliced green onions
1 teaspoon bottled minced garlic
1 teaspoon grated fresh ginger
1 cup orange juice
1 tablespoon white wine vinegar
2 teaspoons cornstarch
¼ cup golden raisins
⅛ teaspoon salt

1. Finely shred ½ teaspoon peel from one of the oranges; set peel aside. Peel and section oranges, discarding seeds. Set orange sections aside.

2. Sprinkle meat with the ¼ teaspoon salt and the pepper. In a large nonstick skillet, heat olive oil over medium-high heat. Add meat; cook for 4 to 6 minutes or until brown, turning once halfway through cooking. Remove meat from skillet, reserving drippings in skillet. Add green onions, garlic, and ginger to drippings in skillet. Cook and stir over medium heat for 1 minute.

3. In a small bowl, stir together orange juice, vinegar, and cornstarch; add to skillet. Cook and stir until slightly thickened and bubbly. Add the orange peel, orange sections, raisins, and the ⅛ teaspoon salt to skillet. Toss gently to coat. Return meat to skillet; spoon sauce over meat. Heat through.

Per serving: 196 cal., 4 g total fat (1 g sat. fat), 66 mg chol., 265 mg sodium, 21 g carb., 2 g fiber, 19 g pro.

Lamb with Spicy Apricot Sauce

Ginger-rubbed lamb and a sweet-hot apricot brush-on stack up to a first-rate entrée that's not for timid taste buds. Present these can't-miss chops with a mixture of hot cooked couscous and peas.

Prep: 15 minutes **Grill:** 12 minutes
Makes 4 servings

4	lamb loin chops, cut 1 inch thick
¼	cup apricot spreadable fruit
2	tablespoons white wine vinegar
2	teaspoons Dijon-style mustard
½	teaspoon ground turmeric
½	teaspoon bottled minced garlic
⅛	teaspoon cayenne pepper
1	tablespoon grated fresh ginger
1	teaspoon olive oil
¼	teaspoon salt

1. Trim fat from chops; set chops aside. In a small bowl, stir together apricot spreadable fruit, white wine vinegar, mustard, turmeric, garlic, and cayenne pepper. Set aside.

2. In another small bowl, stir together ginger, olive oil, and salt. Spoon ginger mixture evenly over chops; rub in with your fingers.

3. Place chops on the rack of an uncovered grill directly over medium coals. Grill to desired doneness, turning once halfway through grilling and brushing with apricot mixture during the last 5 minutes of grilling. Allow 12 to 14 minutes for medium-rare doneness (145°F) or 15 to 17 minutes for medium doneness (160°F). Discard any remaining apricot mixture.

Per serving: 188 cal., 6 g total fat (2 g sat. fat), 60 mg chol., 257 mg sodium, 13 g carb., 0 g fiber, 19 g pro.

Pan-Seared Lamb Chops with Fresh Mint Salad

For the best color and flavor, let the lamb chops cook in the skillet, moving them only once to flip them.

Start to finish: 30 minutes
Makes 4 servings

¼	cup snipped fresh mint
¼	cup snipped fresh flat-leaf parsley
¼	cup crumbled feta cheese (1 ounce)
¼	cup chopped pecans, toasted
8	lamb rib chops or loin chops, cut 1 inch thick (about 2 pounds total)
2	teaspoons olive oil
¼	teaspoon salt
⅛	teaspoon ground black pepper
	Olive oil (optional)
	Lemon juice (optional)
	Salad greens (optional)

1. In a small bowl, combine mint, parsley, feta cheese, and pecans; set aside.

2. Trim fat from chops. Rub chops with the 2 teaspoons olive oil; sprinkle with the salt and pepper. Preheat a large heavy skillet over medium-high heat until very hot. Add chops. Cook for 8 to 10 minutes or until well browned and medium doneness (145°F), turning chops once halfway through cooking.

3. To serve, sprinkle chops with mint mixture. If desired, drizzle additional olive oil and/or lemon juice over mint mixture and serve with salad greens.

Per serving: 252 cal., 17 g total fat (5 g sat. fat), 72 mg chol., 311 mg sodium, 2 g carb., 1 g fiber, 22 g pro.

Pan-Seared Lamb Chops with Fresh Mint Salad

Lamb Chops with Tomatoes

Lamb Chops with Tomatoes

An aromatic balsamic-flavored tomato sauce brings out the best in succulent grilled lamb chops.
Start to finish: 20 minutes
Makes 4 servings

8   lamb loin chops, cut 1 inch thick
    Salt and ground black pepper
1   8.8-ounce pouch cooked long grain rice
4   medium Roma tomatoes, cut up
4   green onions, cut into 1-inch pieces
1   tablespoon snipped fresh oregano
1   tablespoon balsamic vinegar

1.   Season chops with salt and pepper. Place chops on the rack of an uncovered grill directly over medium coals. Grill for 12 to 14 minutes for medium-rare (145°F), turning once halfway through grilling.

2.   Meanwhile, microwave rice according to package directions. In food processor, combine tomatoes, green onions, and oregano; process with on/off turns until coarsely chopped. Transfer to bowl; stir in vinegar. Season with salt and pepper. Arrange chops on rice and top with tomato mixture.

Per serving: 273 cal., 7 g total fat (2 g sat. fat), 70 mg chol., 153 mg sodium, 26 g carbo., 3 g fiber, 25 g pro.

Smoked Pork Chops with Curried Fruit

This is a great dish to make when fresh cranberries come into season.
Start to finish: 20 minutes
Makes 4 servings

4   cooked smoked pork chops, cut ¾ inch thick
1   tablespoon cooking oil
1   8-ounce can pineapple chunks (juice pack)
⅓   cup chopped onion (1 small)
1   tablespoon butter or margarine
1½   teaspoons curry powder
¾   cup orange juice
1   tablespoon cornstarch
1   cup fresh cranberries
1   11-ounce can mandarin orange sections, drained
2   cups hot cooked couscous or basmati rice (optional)

1.   Trim fat from meat. In a 12-inch skillet, cook chops in hot oil for 8 to 10 minutes or until hot, turning once.

2.   Meanwhile, for sauce, drain pineapple, reserving juice. In a medium saucepan, cook onion in hot butter until tender. Stir in curry powder. Cook and stir for 1 minute. Stir together reserved pineapple juice, orange juice, and cornstarch. Stir into saucepan. Add cranberries. Cook and stir over medium heat until thickened and bubbly. Cook and stir for 2 minutes more. Gently stir in pineapple and mandarin oranges; heat through. Serve sauce over pork chops. If desired, serve with couscous or rice.

Per serving: 422 cal., 20 g total fat (7 g sat. fat), 92 mg chol., 2,162 mg sodium, 28 g carbo., 3 g fiber, 33 g pro.

Provolone and Ham Melt

light dinners

When it's hot outside or when you're particularly busy, a light, delicious dinner fits the bill. This tempting collection of time-saving recipes brings you family-pleasing options for sandwiches, soups, and salads. Each one comes together easily and quickly.

Provolone and Ham Melt

Mix and match the ingredients in this sandwich to satisfy both children and adults. For kids, combine cheddar cheese, ham, and apple. Offer grown-ups a mix of provolone cheese, roasted red sweet pepper, and prosciutto.

Prep: 15 minutes   **Cook:** 8 minutes
Makes 4 sandwiches

8   slices thick-cut multigrain, whole wheat, poppy seed, white, or pumpernickel bread
    Butter or margarine, softened
4   teaspoons mayonnaise or salad dressing
4   ounces provolone and/or cheddar cheese, thinly sliced
1   pear or apple, cored and thinly sliced, or 4 canned pineapple rings, well drained and patted dry
⅓   cup roasted red sweet peppers, well drained and cut into strips
4   ounces thinly sliced cooked ham and/or prosciutto
2   tablespoons mango chutney
    Fresh fruit (such as sliced pears and apples, pineapple wedges, or grapes) (optional)

1. Spread one side of each bread slice with butter. Place four of the bread slices, buttered sides down, on a griddle. Spread mayonnaise on the four bread slices on the griddle. Top with cheese, pear or apple slices or pineapple rings, and roasted sweet peppers. Top with ham and/or prosciutto.

2. Cut up any large pieces of chutney; spread the unbuttered sides of the remaining four bread slices with chutney. Place over bread slices on griddle, buttered sides up.

3. Cook sandwiches over medium heat about 8 minutes or until bread is toasted and cheese is melted, turning once halfway through cooking. If desired, serve with additional fruit.

Per sandwich: 466 cal., 22 g total fat (11 g sat. fat), 53 mg chol., 1,085 mg sodium, 48 g carb., 7 g fiber, 20 g pro.

Deli Sandwich Stacks

A creamy cheese-and-honey mustard spread serves as a flavorful base for sliced ham, turkey breast, and Colby-Jack cheese.

Start to finish: 20 minutes
Makes 4 servings

½ of a 4-ounce container light semisoft cheese with garlic and herb

2 tablespoons honey mustard

¼ teaspoon lemon-pepper seasoning

6 slices marble rye, cracked wheat, or seven-grain bread

2 small plum tomatoes, thinly sliced

⅓ cup sliced canned banana peppers, well drained

1 cup loosely packed fresh spinach leaves or 4 lettuce leaves

4 thin slices Colby and Monterey Jack cheese

4 ounces thinly sliced cooked turkey breast

4 ounces low-fat, reduced-sodium thinly sliced cooked ham

1. In a small bowl, combine semisoft cheese, honey mustard, and lemon-pepper seasoning. Spread the cheese mixture evenly onto one side of each of four of the bread slices; lay bread, spread sides up, on work surface.

2. Divide tomatoes, banana peppers, spinach or lettuce, and Colby and Monterey Jack cheese among the four bread slices. Top *two* of the stacks with turkey and *two* of the stacks with ham. Arrange the stacks with ham on top of the stacks with turkey. Top with remaining two bread slices. Cut stacks in half. Secure with wooden picks.

Per serving: 315 cal., 12 g total fat (6 g sat. fat), 51 mg chol., 1,245 mg sodium, 31 g carb., 4 g fiber, 22 g pro.

Fish Sandwich with Orange-Ginger Topper

If you sometimes opt for a fast-food fish sandwich, try this healthier alternative. It's almost as fast as eating out (it takes only 15 minutes) and is twice as tasty.

Start to finish: 15 minutes
Oven: 450°F
Makes 4 sandwiches

4 fresh or frozen fish fillets (such as cod, orange roughy, or pike), about ½ inch thick (about 1 pound total)

Nonstick cooking spray

¼ cup fine dry bread crumbs

¼ teaspoon ground ginger

⅛ teaspoon salt

⅛ teaspoon cayenne pepper

2 tablespoons butter, melted

4 baguette-style rolls, hamburger buns, or kaiser rolls, split and toasted

4 lettuce leaves

Orange-Ginger Topper

1. Preheat oven to 450°F. Thaw fish, if frozen. Rinse fish; pat dry with paper towels. Lightly coat a shallow baking pan with nonstick cooking spray; set aside. In a small bowl, combine bread crumbs, ginger, salt, and cayenne pepper; set aside. Place fish fillets on waxed paper. Brush tops and sides of fish with melted butter; coat tops and sides with crumb mixture.

2. Arrange fish fillets in a single layer, crumb sides up, in prepared baking pan. Bake for 4 to 6 minutes or until fish flakes easily when tested with a fork. To serve, top bottoms of rolls with lettuce. Top with fish and Orange-Ginger Topper. Add roll tops.

Orange-Ginger Topper: Stir together ¼ cup low-fat mayonnaise dressing, 1 teaspoon orange marmalade, and ¼ teaspoon ground ginger.

Per sandwich: 319 cal., 10 g total fat (5 g sat. fat), 68 mg chol., 711 mg sodium, 31 g carb., 2 g fiber, 25 g pro.

Fish Sandwich with Orange-Ginger Topper

Nutty Cucumber Sandwich

Select soft goat cheese that has been rolled in cracked black pepper to add another flavor dimension to this meatless sandwich.

Start to finish: 15 minutes
Makes 4 sandwiches

½	cup fresh snow pea pods, trimmed
½	of a medium cucumber
8	thin slices rye bread
3	to 4 ounces soft goat cheese (chèvre)
⅓	cup seasoned roasted soy nuts (such as ranch or garlic)
1	medium tomato, thinly sliced
	Salt

1. In a covered small saucepan, cook the pea pods in a small amount of boiling lightly salted water for 2 minutes. Drain; rinse pea pods with cold water. Drain again. Place pea pods in a small bowl; chill until needed.

2. Use a vegetable peeler to remove a few lengthwise strips of peel from the cucumber. Thinly slice cucumber.

3. Spread one side of each bread slice with goat cheese. Sprinkle four of the bread slices with soy nuts, gently pressing nuts into the cheese. Top soy nuts with cucumber slices, tomato slices, and pea pods. Sprinkle with salt. Top with remaining bread slices, cheese sides down.

Per sandwich: 276 cal., 9 g total fat (4 g sat. fat), 10 mg chol., 540 mg sodium, 36 g carb., 6 g fiber, 14 g pro.

Meat-and-Cheese Sandwich Loaf

This fuss-free sandwich is terrific for entertaining too. Keep an extra loaf of bread in the freezer and extra cheese and meats in the refrigerator, so on the spur of the moment, you can invite friends to stay for a meal.

Prep: 10 minutes **Bake:** 15 minutes
Oven: 375°F
Makes 6 servings

¼	cup creamy Dijon-style mustard blend
1	tablespoon prepared horseradish
1	unsliced loaf Italian bread (about 12 inches long)
1	6-ounce package Swiss cheese slices
2	2½-ounce packages very thinly sliced smoked chicken or very thinly sliced smoked turkey
1	2½-ounce package very thinly sliced pastrami

1. Preheat oven to 375°F. In a small bowl, stir together the Dijon-style mustard blend and horseradish. Set aside.

2. Cut bread loaf into 1-inch-thick slices by cutting from the top to, but not through, the bottom crust. (You should have 11 pockets.)

3. To assemble sandwich loaf, spread a scant tablespoon of the mustard blend mixture in every other pocket in the bread loaf, starting with the first pocket on one end and spreading mustard blend evenly over both sides of the pocket.

4. Divide cheese slices, smoked chicken or turkey slices, and pastrami slices among the mustard-spread pockets.

5. Place the bread loaf on a baking sheet. Bake about 15 minutes or until heated through.

6. To serve, cut loaf into sandwiches by cutting through the bottom crusts of the unfilled pockets.

Per serving: 394 cal., 15 g total fat (7 g sat. fat), 55 mg chol., 1,058 mg sodium, 42 g carb., 2 g fiber, 21 g pro.

Roast Beef Sandwich with Horseradish Slaw

Horseradish and beef, common sandwich partners, pair up here with a twist, as the horseradish seasons crunchy broccoli slaw.

Start to finish: 15 minutes
Makes 4 sandwiches

⅓	cup light dairy sour cream
2	tablespoons snipped fresh chives
2	tablespoons spicy brown mustard
1	teaspoon prepared horseradish
½	teaspoon sugar
¼	teaspoon salt
1	cup packaged shredded broccoli (broccoli slaw mix)
8	ounces thinly sliced cooked roast beef
8	½-inch-thick slices sourdough bread, toasted

1. In a medium bowl, combine sour cream, chives, brown mustard, horseradish, sugar, and salt. Add shredded broccoli; toss to coat.

2. To assemble, divide roast beef among four of the bread slices. Top with broccoli mixture. Top with the remaining bread slices. If desired, secure the sandwiches with wooden toothpicks.

Per sandwich: 315 cal., 11 g total fat (4 g sat. fat), 53 mg chol., 630 mg sodium, 30 g carb., 2 g fiber, 23 g pro.

Veggie-Cheese Sandwich and Tomato Soup

With this two-in-one recipe, you can have a dynamite soup and sandwich dinner for four ready to serve in only 25 minutes.

Start to finish: 25 minutes
Makes 4 servings

4	½-inch-thick slices country French white bread
4	½-inch-thick slices wheat bread
1	tablespoon olive oil or cooking oil
2	tablespoons honey mustard or mustard
3	to 4 ounces thinly sliced farmer cheese or cheddar cheese
½	cup thinly sliced cucumber
½	cup fresh spinach leaves or shredded broccoli (broccoli slaw mix)
¼	cup thinly sliced red onion
1	32-ounce container ready-to-serve tomato soup
1	cup chopped plum tomatoes (about 3)
1	tablespoon balsamic vinegar
¼	cup plain low-fat yogurt
1	tablespoon snipped fresh chives

1. For sandwiches: Brush one side of each bread slice lightly with oil. Brush other side of each bread slice with honey mustard. Lay the French bread slices, mustard sides up, on work surface. Top with cheese. Top cheese with cucumber, spinach, and red onion. Top with wheat bread slices, mustard sides down.

2. Preheat an indoor electric grill or preheat a large skillet over medium heat. Place the sandwiches on the grill rack. If using a covered grill, close lid. Grill sandwiches until bread is golden brown and cheese is melted. (For a covered grill, allow 3 to 5 minutes. For an uncovered grill or skillet, allow 6 to 8 minutes, turning once halfway through grilling.) Cut each sandwich into quarters.

3. Meanwhile, for soup: In a medium saucepan, stir together tomato soup, chopped plum tomatoes, and balsamic vinegar. Heat through. Top individual servings with yogurt; swirl slightly. Sprinkle individual servings with chives. Serve the sandwiches with the soup.

Per serving: 365 cal., 10 g total fat (3 g sat. fat), 14 mg chol., 1,200 mg sodium, 58 g carb., 5 g fiber, 12 g pro.

Turkey and Rice Soup

Serve crispy breadsticks with this meal-in-a-bowl.

Start to finish: 25 minutes
Makes 6 servings

2	14-ounce cans reduced-sodium chicken broth
1½	cups water
1	teaspoon snipped fresh rosemary or ¼ teaspoon dried rosemary, crushed
¼	teaspoon ground black pepper
1	medium carrot, thinly sliced
1	stalk celery, thinly sliced
1	small onion, thinly sliced
1	cup quick-cooking rice
½	cup loose-pack frozen cut green beans
2	cups chopped cooked turkey or chicken (about 10 ounces)
1	14½-ounce can diced tomatoes, undrained Fresh rosemary sprigs (optional)

1. In a large saucepan, combine broth, the water, snipped or dried rosemary, and pepper. Add carrot, celery, and onion. Bring to boiling.

2. Stir in uncooked rice and green beans. Return to boiling; reduce heat. Cover and simmer for 10 to 12 minutes or until vegetables are tender. Stir in turkey and undrained tomatoes; heat through. If desired, garnish with rosemary sprigs.

Per serving: 177 cal., 2 g total fat (1 g sat. fat), 35 mg chol., 500 mg sodium, 20 g carb., 1 g fiber, 17 g pro.

Turkey and Rice Soup

This refreshing, surprisingly simple
medley of elbow macaroni, shrimp, and creamy
onion salad dressing is served on a bed of spinach
—making it healthy and satisfying.

Spinach-Pasta Salad with Shrimp

Spinach-Pasta Salad with Shrimp

If you prefer, make the pasta-and-shrimp mixture up to 24 hours ahead and chill it. Then toss it with the spinach and goat cheese just before serving.

Start to finish: 25 minutes
Makes 6 servings

- 1 **cup dried elbow macaroni or tiny shell macaroni**
- 1 **pound frozen cooked shrimp, thawed, or 1 pound cooked peeled and deveined shrimp (from supermarket deli)**
- 1 **cup chopped red sweet pepper (from supermarket salad bar)**
- ⅓ **cup bottled creamy onion or Caesar salad dressing**
- 2 **tablespoons snipped fresh dill (optional)**
  Salt
  Freshly ground black pepper
- 1 **6-ounce package baby spinach**
- 4 **ounces goat cheese (chèvre), sliced, or feta cheese, crumbled**

1. Cook macaroni according to package directions. Drain well. Rinse with cold water; drain again.

2. In an extra-large bowl, combine the cooked macaroni, shrimp, and sweet pepper. Drizzle with salad dressing. If desired, sprinkle with dill. Toss to coat. Season to taste with salt and black pepper.

3. Divide spinach mixture among six salad plates or bowls. Top with shrimp mixture and cheese.

Per serving: 247 cal., 10 g total fat (4 g sat. fat), 156 mg chol., 435 mg sodium, 17 g carb., 2 g fiber, 23 g pro.

Quick Pork-Bean Soup

Round out your meal with crusty rolls and creamy coleslaw from the deli.

Prep: 15 minutes   **Cook:** 15 minutes
Makes 4 servings

- 12 **ounces lean boneless pork**
- 1 **large onion, chopped**
- 2 **tablespoons cooking oil**
- 2 **cups water**
- 1 **11½-ounce can condensed bean with bacon soup**
- 3 **medium carrots, sliced**
- 1 **teaspoon Worcestershire sauce**
- ¼ **teaspoon dry mustard**

1. Cut pork into thin bite-size strips. In a large skillet, cook pork and onion in hot oil for 3 to 4 minutes or until pork is browned. Stir in the water, bean with bacon soup, carrots, Worcestershire sauce, and dry mustard.

2. Bring to boiling; reduce heat. Cover and simmer for 15 minutes.

Per serving: 312 cal., 13 g total fat (3 g sat. fat), 52 mg chol., 678 mg sodium, 23 g carb., 6 g fiber, 24 g pro.

Visit a Salad Bar

Relying on precut fruits and vegetables from your supermarket's salad bar can save you precious minutes in the kitchen. When a recipe calls for chopped sweet pepper, sliced mushrooms, broccoli or cauliflower florets, melon chunks, ready-to-eat strawberries, or other cut-up fruits or vegetables, picking up these items at the salad bar not only shortcuts preparation time but allows you to purchase just the amount you need with no leftovers.

Tuna Chowder

Just a little bit of thyme and a sprinkling of cooked bacon add loads of flavor to this simple fix-up for canned potato soup.

Start to finish: 25 minutes
Makes 4 servings

4 slices bacon
1 medium green sweet pepper, chopped
1 small onion, chopped
3 cups milk
2 10¾-ounce cans condensed cream of potato soup
½ teaspoon dried thyme, crushed
2 6-ounce cans tuna, drained and flaked

1. In a large skillet, cook bacon until crisp. Drain, reserving drippings. Crumble bacon and set aside.

2. In the same skillet, cook sweet pepper and onion in reserved drippings until tender. Stir in milk, cream of potato soup, and thyme; bring just to boiling. Gently stir in tuna; heat through. Sprinkle individual servings with crumbled bacon.

Per serving: 435 cal., 18 g total fat (7 g sat. fat), 49 mg chol., 1,651 mg sodium, 30 g carb., 2 g fiber, 36 g pro.

Count on Couscous

An easy no-fuss way to add variety to meals is to keep quick-cooking couscous on hand. Available plain and with seasonings, couscous is a tiny grain-shape pasta-like product made from semolina flour. Once cooked and fluffed up, it's good served as a side dish stand-in for rice or polenta. Look for it in the rice and dry bean section of your supermarket.

Couscous Chicken Salad

Handy refrigerated lemon-pepper or Italian-style chicken breast strips save you the work and time of cutting up, seasoning, and cooking your own chicken.

Start to finish: 15 minutes
Makes 4 servings

1 14-ounce can chicken broth
1¼ cups quick-cooking couscous
½ cup mango chutney, large pieces cut up
¼ cup bottled olive oil and vinegar salad dressing, white wine vinaigrette salad dressing, or roasted garlic vinaigrette salad dressing
1 6-ounce package cooked, refrigerated lemon-pepper or Italian-style chicken breast strips, cut into bite-size pieces (about 1½ cups)
½ cup golden raisins or raisins (optional)
1 cup coarsely chopped radishes or seeded cucumber
Salt
Freshly ground black pepper
1 small cucumber, cut into spears

1. In a medium saucepan, bring chicken broth to boiling. Stir in couscous. Cover and remove from heat. Let stand for 5 minutes. Fluff couscous lightly with a fork.

2. In a medium bowl, combine mango chutney and salad dressing. Add chicken, raisins (if desired), chopped radishes, and cooked couscous. Toss to coat. Season to taste with salt and pepper. Serve with cucumber spears.

Per serving: 411 cal., 10 g total fat (2 g sat. fat), 22 mg chol., 848 mg sodium, 63 g carb., 4 g fiber, 16 g pro.

Mango chutney adds a **big hit of spicy-sweet flavor** to ready-in-minutes couscous and tender seasoned bites of chicken. **Pick up some muffins or crackers** at the supermarket to serve with the salad.

Couscous Chicken Salad

Quick-Fried Chicken Salad with Strawberries

These **chicken breast strips** double-dipped
in a lemon-and-herb-seasoned flour mixture and
flash-fried have all the **crunch of
traditional fried chicken.**

Quick-Fried Chicken Salad with Strawberries

When strawberries are out of season, use refrigerated mango or papaya chunks instead.

Start to finish: 30 minutes
Makes 6 servings

¾ cup all-purpose flour
4 tablespoons snipped fresh basil
1 tablespoon finely shredded lemon peel
2 eggs, beaten
1 pound skinless, boneless chicken breast strips
2 tablespoons cooking oil
4 cups mixed spring salad greens
1 head radicchio, torn into bite-size pieces
2 cups sliced fresh strawberries
½ cup bottled balsamic vinaigrette salad dressing
6 butterhead (Boston or Bibb) lettuce leaves

1. In a shallow dish, combine flour, 2 tablespoons of the snipped basil, and the lemon peel. Place eggs in another shallow dish. Dip chicken into flour mixture, then into the eggs, and then again into flour mixture to coat.

2. In a heavy 12-inch skillet, heat cooking oil over medium-high heat. Add chicken strips to skillet. Cook for 6 to 8 minutes or until chicken is no longer pink, turning once. (If necessary to prevent overbrowning, reduce heat to medium. Add more oil as needed during cooking.) Cool slightly.

3. Meanwhile, in a large bowl, toss together salad greens, radicchio, strawberries, and the remaining 2 tablespoons snipped basil. Drizzle vinaigrette over greens mixture; toss gently to coat. To serve, line six individual bowls with lettuce leaves. Add greens mixture. Top with chicken.

Per serving: 261 cal., 13 g total fat (2 g sat. fat), 79 mg chol., 295 mg sodium, 16 g carb., 2 g fiber, 21 g pro.

Three-Herb Deviled Eggs

These lunchtime favorites are a star at dinnertime or at your next party. Chop up the leftover egg tops to use in a chef's salad or egg salad.

Start to finish: 30 minutes
Makes 6 servings

12 hard-cooked eggs,* peeled
¼ cup mayonnaise or salad dressing
¼ cup dairy sour cream
2 to 3 teaspoons Dijon-style mustard
2 tablespoons snipped fresh parsley
2 tablespoons snipped fresh dill or 1½ teaspoons dried dill
2 tablespoons snipped fresh chives
  Sea salt or salt
  Freshly ground black pepper
  Paprika or cayenne pepper (optional)

1. Cut the top off each of the hard-cooked eggs about one-third from the top; scoop out yolk. Cut a small thin slice off the rounded bottom of each so it sits flat. If desired, chill tops for another use.

2. Place yolks in a bowl; mash with a fork. Add mayonnaise, sour cream, and mustard; mix well. Stir in parsley, dill, and chives. Season to taste with salt and black pepper. Stuff egg yolk mixture into egg whites. If desired, sprinkle tops with paprika or cayenne pepper.

Per serving: 213 cal., 16 g total fat (5 g sat. fat), 430 mg chol., 305 mg sodium, 4 g carb., 0 g fiber, 13 g pro.

*****Test Kitchen Tip:** To save time, purchase hard-cooked eggs at your supermarket's deli. Or cook the eggs ahead. To hard-cook eggs, place 12 eggs in a single layer in a large Dutch oven. Add just enough cold water to cover the eggs. Bring to a rapid boil over high heat. Remove from heat; cover and let stand for 15 minutes. Drain. Place eggs in ice water until cool enough to handle; drain. To peel, gently tap each egg on countertop. Roll egg between the palms of your hands. Peel off shell, starting at the large end. Cover and chill until ready to use (up to 24 hours).

Pesto Turkey Soup

All the goods for this hearty soup keep well in the fridge and pantry. Have them ready for a satisfying meal when the weather cools and a steaming bowl of soup sounds divine.

Start to finish: 20 minutes
Makes 6 servings

- 4 cups chicken broth
- ¼ teaspoon dried Italian seasoning, crushed
- ¼ teaspoon ground black pepper
- 1 10-ounce package frozen mixed vegetables (2 cups)
- 1 cup quick-cooking white or brown rice
- 2 cups chopped cooked turkey or chicken
- 1 14.5-ounce can diced tomatoes, drained
- 2 tablespoons purchased basil pesto

1. In a large saucepan, combine broth, Italian seasoning, and pepper. Bring to boiling. Stir in mixed vegetables and rice. Return to boiling; reduce heat. Simmer, covered, for 8 to 10 minutes or until vegetables are tender. Stir in turkey, drained tomatoes, and pesto; heat through.

Per serving: 233 cal., 6 g total fat (1 g sat. fat), 38 mg chol., 847 mg sodium, 25 g carbo., 2 g fiber, 18 g pro.

Creamy Pesto Turkey Soup: Prepare as above, except in a small bowl whisk together one 8-ounce carton dairy sour cream and 2 tablespoons all-purpose flour. Stir into soup. Cook and stir until thickened and bubbly. Cook and stir 1 minute more.

Best Pesto

Prepared pesto can be purchased in both jars and in plastic tubs in the refrigerated section of your supermarket—often in a specialty case with fresh pastas and tomato and Alfredo sauce. While either type works equally well in most recipes, your best bet for quality is the refrigerated type—it keeps its green color and bright taste longer than the jarred type.

Shore Chowder

Prep: 20 minutes **Cook:** 9 minutes
Makes 4 servings

- ¼ cup lime mayonnaise*
- 2 cloves minced garlic
- 1 14-ounce can reduced-sodium chicken broth
- 4 small carrots, peeled and cut into thin strips or 1½ cups packaged fresh carrot strips
- 1½ cups purchased puttanesca pasta sauce
- 1 cup grape tomatoes
- 1 pound fresh or frozen skinless fish fillets, such as cod, sole, or striped bass, thawed and cut into 2-inch pieces
- 2 cups fresh baby spinach
  Sliced baguette-style French bread or French bread, toasted if desired

1. In a small bowl, combine lime mayonnaise and garlic; set aside.

2. In a 3-quart microwave-safe bowl, combine chicken broth and carrots. Cover and microwave on 100% power (high) for 4 to 5 minutes or until crisp-tender, stirring once.

3. Uncover carrot mixture. Stir in puttanesca sauce, tomatoes, and fish. Cover and microwave on high for 3 to 4 minutes or until fish just begins to flake easily, stirring once. Stir in spinach. Ladle fish and vegetables into individual bowls. Pass mayonnaise mixture with bread slices to serve with chowder.

*Test Kitchen Tip: Find lime mayonnaise in the Hispanic food section of supermarkets or in Hispanic markets. For a substitution, combine mayonnaise with 1/4 teaspoon finely shredded lime peel.

Per serving: 380 cal., 16 g total fat (2 g sat. fat), 64 mg chol., 1,168 mg sodium, 28 g carbo., 5 g fiber, 26 g pro.

Shore Chowder

Take your taste buds to the shore with **soup that simmers in minutes.** Purchased puttanesca pasta sauce is the shortcut ingredient that adds **character and punch.**

Quick Cioppino

San Francisco's Italian immigrants are credited with creating the original cioppino (chuh-PEE-noh), a tasty fish and shellfish stew. This simplified version features canned tomatoes and quick-cooking cod and shrimp.

Start to finish: 20 minutes
Makes 4 servings (5½ cups)

1	medium green sweet pepper, cut into thin bite-size strips
1	large onion, chopped (1 cup)
2	cloves garlic, minced
1	tablespoon olive oil or cooking oil
2	14.5-ounce cans Italian-style stewed tomatoes, undrained
½	cup water
6	ounces fresh cod fillets, cut into 1-inch pieces
6	ounces peeled and deveined fresh shrimp
3	tablespoons snipped fresh basil

1. In a large saucepan, cook sweet pepper, onion, and garlic in hot oil until tender. Stir in undrained tomatoes and the water. Bring to boiling.

2. Stir in cod and shrimp. Return to boiling; reduce heat. Simmer, covered, for 2 to 3 minutes or until the cod flakes easily and shrimp are opaque. Stir in basil.

Per serving: 176 cal., 4 g total fat (1 g sat. fat), 82 mg chol., 819 mg sodium, 19 g carbo., 1 g fiber, 17 g pro.

Tuna Types

Canned tuna comes packed two ways—in water and in oil. Depending on your culinary and dietary preferences, you can use either one. Tuna packed in oil has a slighty better flavor, while tuna packed in water has a slightly higher omega-3 fatty acid content.

Tuna Salad with Capers

The lemon-tarragon mayonnaise gives this delicious tuna salad a refreshing twist. If tarragon is not to your taste, try other fresh herbs such as dill or chervil.

Start to finish: 20 minutes
Makes 6 servings

½	cup mayonnaise or salad dressing
2	tablespoons capers, drained
2	tablespoons lemon juice
1	tablespoon snipped fresh tarragon
1	teaspoon Cajun seasoning
1	12-ounce can solid white tuna
2	tablespoons milk
1	10-ounce package torn mixed greens (romaine blend) or 8 cups torn romaine
2	cups shredded cabbage with carrot (coleslaw mix)
2	small tomatoes, cut into wedges

1. In a small bowl, combine mayonnaise, capers, lemon juice, and tarragon. Set aside. In a large bowl flake tuna into large chunks; toss with 3 tablespoons of the mayonnaise mixture. Stir milk into remaining mayonnaise mixture.

2. Divide greens among six plates; top with shredded cabbage, tuna, and tomato wedges. Serve with dressing.

Per serving: 228 cal., 17 g total fat (3 g sat. fat), 38 mg chol., 455 mg sodium, 5 g carbo., 2 g fiber, 15 g pro.

Tuna Salad with Capers

Shrimp and Asparagus Salad

Shrimp and Asparagus Salad

The fleshy green spears of asparagus, the peppery tang of watercress, and fruity vinaigrette dressing make this speedy shrimp salad a sensational mixture of tastes and textures.

Start to finish: 15 minutes
Makes 4 servings

- 1 bunch (12 to 16 ounces) fresh asparagus spears, trimmed
- 4 cups watercress, tough stems removed
- 1 16-ounce package frozen peeled, cooked shrimp with tails intact, thawed
- 2 cups cherry tomatoes, halved
- ½ cup bottled light raspberry or berry vinaigrette salad dressing
  Cracked black pepper
  Cracker bread (optional)

1. In a large skillet, cook asparagus, covered, in a small amount of boiling lightly salted water for 3 minutes or until crisp-tender; drain in a colander. Run under cold water until cool.

2. Divide asparagus among four dinner plates; top with watercress, shrimp, and cherry tomatoes. Drizzle with dressing. Sprinkle with cracked black pepper and, if desired, serve wtih cracker bread.
Per serving: 257 cal., 8 g total fat (1 g sat. fat), 227 mg chol., 360 mg sodium, 14 g carbo., 2 g fiber, 33 g pro.

Shrimp-Avocado Hoagies

Dinner alfresco calls for a fresh-tasting meal in a roll, such as this one. And the coolest part is the 15-minute prep time.

Start to finish: 15 minutes
Makes 4 servings

- 1 10- to 12-ounce package frozen peeled, cooked shrimp, thawed and coarsely chopped
- 2 large avocados, pitted, peeled, and chopped
- ½ cup shredded carrot (1 medium)
- ⅓ cup bottled coleslaw salad dressing
- 4 6-inch ciabatta rolls or hoagie buns, split
  Lemon wedges (optional)

1. In a large bowl, combine shrimp, avocados, carrot, and salad dressing. Using a spoon, slightly hollow bottoms and tops of rolls, leaving 12-inch shell. Discard excess bread. Toast buns. Spoon shrimp mixture into rolls. If desired, serve with lemon wedges.
Per serving: 560 cal., 24 g total fat (4 g sat. fat), 144 mg chol., 825 mg sodium, 63 g carbo., 8 g fiber, 25 g pro.

Berry-Nut French Toast

breakfast
for dinner

Sometimes after a long hard day, you just want comforting, simple breakfast food—so flip-flop your meals and maybe a pancake or two. From French toast and pancakes, to eggs Benedict and omelets, to hash browns and hot chocolate, you'll find everything you need to create flavor-packed family meals in minutes.

Berry-Nut French Toast

Cereal studded with cranberries and almonds makes a flavorful and crispy coating for thick slices of French or Italian bread in this sure-to-please dish.

Start to finish: 15 minutes
Makes 2 servings

2   **cups multigrain flakes with oat clusters, cranberries, and almonds**
4   **eggs**
½   **teaspoon ground cinnamon**
¼   **teaspoon ground nutmeg**
4   **¾-inch-thick slices French or Italian bread**
2   **tablespoons butter**
    Fruit-flavored syrup, maple syrup, or apricot preserves, warmed

1. Coarsely crush the cereal and place in a shallow dish. Set aside.

2. In another shallow dish, whisk together eggs, cinnamon, and nutmeg until well mixed. Dip bread slices into egg mixture until moistened, turning to coat; dip in crushed cereal, turning to coat.

3. In a large skillet or on a griddle, melt butter over medium-low heat. Add bread slices; cook about 4 minutes or until golden brown, turning once. Serve with warm syrup or preserves.

Per serving: 606 cal., 27 g total fat (11 g sat. fat), 458 mg chol., 765 mg sodium, 72 g carb., 5 g fiber, 21 g pro.

Banana-Pecan Waffles

Banana-Pecan Waffles

The waffles are done when steam stops escaping from the sides of the baker or when the indicator light comes on.

Prep: 20 minutes **Cook:** 3 to 4 minutes per waffle
Makes about 9 waffles

1¾	cups all-purpose flour
2	tablespoons sugar
1	tablespoon baking powder
½	teaspoon ground cinnamon
¼	teaspoon salt
2	small bananas, mashed (¾ cup)
2	eggs
1	cup milk
¼	cup cooking oil or melted butter
1	teaspoon vanilla
½	cup finely chopped pecans, toasted and cooled
	Butter, maple syrup, caramel ice cream topping, sliced bananas, and/or chopped, toasted pecans (optional)

1. In a large bowl, stir together flour, sugar, baking powder, cinnamon and salt.

2. In medium bowl, beat together banana and eggs. Stir in milk, cooking oil, and vanilla. Add banana mixture all at once to the flour mixture. Stir just until moistened (batter should be slightly lumpy). Stir in ½ cup pecans.

3. Add batter to a preheated, lightly greased waffle baker according to manufacturer's directions. Close lid quickly; do not open until done. Bake according to manufacturer's directions. When done, use a fork to lift waffle off grid. Repeat with remaining batter. Serve warm* with desired toppings.

Per serving: 241 cal., 12 g total fat (2 g. sat. fat), 49 mg chol., 172 mg sodium, 28 g carbo., 2 g fiber, 5 g pro.

*Test Kitchen Tip: Keep prepared waffles warm in a 300°F oven while baking the other waffles.

Shredded Potatoes with Sausage and Apples

Frozen hash brown potatoes make this skillet meal a snap to prepare. For a healthier entrée, choose a lean or low-fat sausage and leave the apple unpeeled.

Start to finish: 30 minutes
Makes 4 servings

2	tablespoons olive oil
2	tablespoons butter
½	of a 26-ounce package frozen shredded hash brown potatoes (about 5 cups)
1	tablespoon snipped fresh thyme or 1 teaspoon dried thyme, crushed
¼	teaspoon ground black pepper
6	ounces cooked smoked sausage, coarsely chopped
1	medium apple, such as Golden Delicious, cut into thin wedges
	Salt to taste

1. In a 10-inch cast-iron or nonstick skillet, heat the oil and 1 tablespoon of the butter over medium heat. Add potatoes in an even layer. Cook for 8 minutes, stirring occasionally, until lightly browned. Stir in half the thyme and the black pepper. With a wide metal spatula press potatoes down firmly. Cook about 8 minutes more or until potatoes are tender.

2. Meanwhile, in a medium skillet, melt the remaining 1 tablespoon butter over medium heat. Add sausage and apple. Cook about 10 minutes or until apple is tender, stirring occasionally. Stir in remaining thyme.

3. Cut potato mixture into 4 wedges and place on serving plates; top wedges with apple mixture. Add salt to taste.

Per serving: 365 cal., 28 g total fat (10 g sat. fat), 47 mg chol., 381 mg sodium, 21 g carbo., 2 g fiber, 8 g pro.

Tex-Mex Spinach Omelet

Tex-Mex Spinach Omelet

Cilantro adds distinctive flavor to the zesty corn-pepper relish filling. Make extra relish to serve another time over brats, burgers, or hot dogs.

Start to finish: 25 minutes
Makes 2 servings

  4 eggs
  1 tablespoon snipped fresh cilantro
     Dash salt
     Dash ground cumin
     Nonstick cooking spray
  1 ounce cheddar cheese, Swiss cheese, or
     Monterey Jack cheese with jalapeño
     peppers, shredded (¼ cup)
  ¾ cup fresh baby spinach leaves
     Corn-Pepper Relish

1. In a medium bowl, combine egg, cilantro, salt, and cumin. Beat with a whisk or rotary beater until frothy.

2. Coat an unheated 10-inch nonstick skillet with flared sides with nonstick cooking spray. Heat skillet over medium heat.

3. Pour egg mixture into prepared skillet. Cook, without stirring, for 2 to 3 minutes or until egg mixture begins to set. Run a spatula around edge of skillet, lifting egg mixture so uncooked portion flows underneath.

4. Continue cooking and lifting edge until egg mixture is set but is still glossy and moist. Sprinkle with cheese. Top with three-fourths of the spinach and half of the Corn-Pepper Relish. Using the spatula, lift and fold an edge of the omelet partially over filling. Top with remaining spinach and the remaining relish. Cut omelet in half; transfer to warm plates.

Per serving: 230 cal., 14 g total fat (6 g sat. fat), 435 mg chol., 298 mg sodium, 8 g carbo., 1 g fiber, 17 g pro.

Corn-Pepper Relish: In a small bowl, combine ¼ cup chopped red sweet pepper; ¼ cup frozen loose-pack whole kernel corn, thawed; 2 tablespoons chopped red onion; and 1 tablespoon snipped fresh cilantro.

Potato-Vegetable Frittata

Slip this colorful egg dish under the broiler to make the top crisp and crusty. Whether you prepare it for brunch, lunch, or supper, it's supereasy.

Start to finish: 30 minutes
Makes 4 servings

  2 cups broccoli florets
  1 red sweet pepper, cut into bite-size strips
  2 tablespoons olive oil
  ½ of a 20-ounce package refrigerated
     Southwest-style shredded hash brown
     potatoes (2¼ cups)
  8 eggs, lightly beaten
  ¼ teaspoon salt
  ⅛ teaspoon ground black pepper
  2 ounces shredded Colby and Monterey Jack
     cheese (½ cup)
  1 medium tomato, chopped

1. In a large broilerproof skillet, cook broccoli and sweet pepper in oil over medium heat for 2 minutes. Add potatoes. Press into an even layer; cook for 2 minutes. Stir and press again; cook 2 minutes more.

2. Preheat broiler. In a large bowl, whisk together eggs, salt, and pepper. Pour over mixture in skillet. As mixture sets, run a spatula round edge of skillet, lifting egg mixture so uncooked portion flows underneath. Continue cooking and lifting edges until egg mixture is almost set but still moist.

3. Broil 4 to 5 inches from heat for 1 to 2 minutes or until top is set. Sprinkle with cheese and tomato; cut into wedges.

Per serving: 354 cal., 22 g total fat (7 g sat. fat), 437 mg chol., 461 mg sodium, 22 g carbo., 3 g fiber, 20 g pro.

Oven Omelets with Artichokes and Spinach

Instead of making individual omelets, bake an entire batch all at once. The artichoke and spinach filling is an appealing change of pace from traditional omelet fillings.

Start to finish: 25 minutes **Oven:** 400°F
Makes 6 servings

	Nonstick cooking spray
10	eggs
¼	cup water
½	teaspoon salt
¼	teaspoon ground black pepper
2	6-ounce jars marinated artichoke hearts, drained and chopped
4	cups chopped fresh spinach
¾	cup shredded Swiss or provolone cheese (3 ounces)

1. Preheat oven to 400°F. Lightly coat a 15x10x1-inch baking pan with cooking spray; set pan aside.

2. In a medium bowl, beat eggs, water, salt, and pepper until combined but not frothy.

3. Place the prepared pan on an oven rack. Carefully pour the egg mixture into the pan. Bake about 7 minutes or until egg mixture is set but still has a glossy surface.

4. Meanwhile, for filling, in a large skillet, cook artichoke hearts over medium heat until heated through, stirring occasionally. Add spinach; cook and stir until spinach wilts.

5. Cut baked egg mixture into six 5-inch square omelets. Remove squares from pan using a large spatula. Invert squares onto warm serving plates.

6. Spoon filling on half of each omelet square. Sprinkle with cheese. Fold the other omelet half over the filled half, forming a triangle or rectangle.

Per serving: 225 cal., 16 g total fat (5 g sat. fat), 367 mg chol., 342 mg sodium, 7 g carbo., 2 g fiber, 16 g pro.

Breakfast Tortilla Wraps

Start to finish: 15 minutes
Makes 4 servings

2	strips bacon, chopped
½	cup chopped green sweet pepper
½	teaspoon ground cumin
¼	teaspoon salt (optional)
¼	teaspoon crushed red pepper (optional)
4	eggs, beaten, or 1 cup refrigerated egg product
½	cup chopped tomato
	Several dashes bottled hot pepper sauce (optional)
4	8-inch flour tortillas, warmed*

1. In a large nonstick skillet, cook bacon until crisp. Drain all but 1 tablespoon of the fat from skillet.

2. Add green pepper, cumin, and, if desired, salt and crushed red pepper to skillet. Cook for 3 minutes.

3. Add eggs or egg product; With a spatula or a large spoon, lift and fold egg mixture so that uncooked portion flows underneath. Continue cooking over medium heat about 2 minutes or until egg is cooked through but still glossy and moist. Stir in tomato and, if desired, hot pepper sauce.

4. Spoon egg mixture onto tortillas and roll up.

Per serving: 193 cal., 9 g total fat (3 g sat. fat), 216 mg chol., 285 mg sodium, 17 g carbo., 1 g fiber, 10 g pro.

*Test Kitchen Tip: To warm tortillas, wrap stack of tortillas tightly in foil. Heat in 350°F oven for 10 minutes. Or, place tortillas between paper towels and microwave on 100% power (high) for 20 to 30 seconds.

Give a new spin to this **bacon and egg combo** by using flavored tortillas. Try **herb, spinach, dried tomato,** or whole wheat.

Breakfast Tortilla Wraps

This **cheesy ham-and-egg skillet** needs nothing more than some **fresh fruit to complete the meal.**

Ham and Potato Scramble

Ham and Potato Scramble

To eliminate some of the chopping, look for packages of diced cooked ham in your supermarket's meat case.

Start to finish: 25 minutes
Makes 4 servings

- 8   **eggs**
- ¼   **cup milk**
- ¼   **teaspoon garlic salt**
- ¼   **teaspoon ground black pepper**
- ¼   **cup thinly sliced green onions**
- 1   **tablespoon butter or margarine**
- 1   **cup refrigerated shredded hash brown potatoes**
- ½   **cup diced cooked ham (about 2 ounces)**
- ⅓   **cup shredded cheddar cheese**

1. In a medium bowl, combine eggs, milk, garlic salt, and pepper; beat with a rotary beater or whisk until well mixed. Stir in green onions. Set aside.

2. In a large nonstick skillet, melt butter over medium heat. Add potatoes and ham to skillet; cook for 6 to 8 minutes or until light brown, stirring occasionally. Add egg mixture. Cook over medium heat, without stirring, until mixture begins to set on the bottom and around edge.

3. Using a large spatula, lift and fold the partially cooked egg mixture so the uncooked portion flows underneath. Continue cooking and folding for 2 to 3 minutes more or until egg mixture is cooked through but is still glossy and moist. Remove from heat immediately. Sprinkle with shredded cheese. Serve warm.

Per serving: 289 cal., 18 g total fat (8 g sat. fat), 453 mg chol., 540 mg sodium, 11 g carb., 1 g fiber, 20 g pro.

Lemon Poppy Seed Pancakes with Raspberry Syrup

Starting with lemon poppy seed muffin mix lets you make these fluffy griddle cakes in a flash.

Start to finish: 20 minutes
Makes 4 servings (8 pancakes)

- 2   **eggs**
- ⅔   **cup milk**
- 1   **7.6-ounce package lemon poppy seed muffin mix**
- 1   **10-ounce package frozen red raspberries in syrup, thawed**
- 2   **teaspoons cornstarch**

1. In a medium bowl, beat together eggs and milk. Add the muffin mix all at once. Stir just until moistened (batter should be nearly smooth).

2. For each pancake, pour or spread *about* ¼ cup of the batter into a 4-inch circle onto a hot, lightly greased griddle or heavy skillet. Cook over medium heat for 1½ to 2 minutes on each side or until pancakes are brown, turning to second sides when pancakes have bubbly surfaces and edges are slightly dry.

3. Meanwhile, for raspberry syrup: In a small saucepan, combine undrained raspberries and cornstarch. Cook and stir until thickened and bubbly. Serve over the pancakes.

Per serving (2 pancakes): 404 cal., 10 g total fat (3 g sat. fat), 114 mg chol., 387 mg sodium, 70 g carb., 3 g fiber, 8 g pro.

Super Syrup

For a quick-as-a-wink meal with a homemade touch, serve your favorite frozen pancakes, waffles, or French toast with the irresistible quick-fixing raspberry syrup from the recipe above.

Shredded Hash Browns

If you like, use frozen chopped onion to shortcut preparation time.
Start to finish: 25 minutes
Makes 2 or 3 servings

3   or 4 small russet or white potatoes (about 12 ounces total)
¼   cup finely chopped onion
1   small fresh jalapeño chile pepper, banana pepper, or Anaheim chile pepper, seeded and chopped (optional)
¼   teaspoon salt
⅛   teaspoon coarsely ground black pepper
2   tablespoons butter, cooking oil, or margarine
    Fresh sage leaves (optional)

1. Peel potatoes and coarsely shred using the coarsest side of the shredder (you should have about 2 cups shredded potatoes). Rinse shredded potatoes in a colander; drain well and pat dry with paper towels. In a medium bowl, combine shredded potatoes, onion, chile pepper (if desired), salt, and black pepper.

2. In a large nonstick skillet, melt butter over medium heat. Carefully add potato mixture, pressing into an even pancakelike round (7 to 8 inches in diameter). Using a spatula, press potato mixture firmly. Cover and cook over medium heat about 8 minutes or until golden brown. Check occasionally and reduce heat, if necessary, to prevent overbrowning.

3. Using two spatulas or a spatula and fork, turn the hash browns. (If you're not sure you can turn in a single flip, cut into quarters and turn by sections.) Cook, uncovered, for 5 to 7 minutes more or until golden brown and crisp. Remove from skillet; cut into wedges. If desired, garnish with fresh sage.
Per serving: 168 cal., 9 g total fat (1 g sat. fat), 0 mg chol., 197 mg sodium, 19 g carb., 2 g fiber, 3 g pro.

Warm Citrus Fruit with Brown Sugar

Be sure to use broiler-safe bakeware for this refreshing compote.
Prep: 15 minutes   **Broil:** 5 minutes
Makes 4 servings

2   medium red grapefruit, peeled and sectioned, or 1½ cups refrigerated grapefruit sections, drained
2   medium oranges, peeled and sectioned
1   cup fresh pineapple chunks or one 8-ounce can pineapple chunks, drained
¼   cup packed brown sugar
2   tablespoons butter, softened

1. Preheat broiler. In a medium bowl, combine grapefruit, oranges, and pineapple. Transfer to a 1-quart broiler-safe au gratin dish or casserole.

2. In a small bowl, stir together brown sugar and butter until well mixed; sprinkle over fruit. Broil about 4 inches from the heat for 5 to 6 minutes or until sugar is bubbly.
Per serving: 192 cal., 6 g total fat (4 g sat. fat), 16 mg chol., 68 mg sodium, 35 g carb., 4 g fiber, 2 g pro.

Shredded Hash Browns

Fiery jalapeño pepper and a liberal sprinkling of ground black pepper add zip to the delicate shreds of fried potatoes. **Hash browns never tasted so good!**

Quick Eggs Benedict

Quick Eggs Benedict

Instead of using the traditional hollandaise sauce, this speedy rendition of the breakfast classic saves time by substituting a seasoned sour cream sauce.

Start to finish: 20 minutes
Makes 4 servings

¼	cup dairy sour cream or crème fraîche
1	teaspoon lemon juice
¾	to 1 teaspoon dry mustard
3	to 4 teaspoons milk
4	eggs
4	½-inch-thick slices crusty French bread or French bread, lightly toasted
4	ounces thinly sliced smoked salmon or 4 slices Canadian-style bacon
	Diced red sweet pepper (optional)
	Salt
	Ground black pepper

1. In a small bowl, combine sour cream, lemon juice, and dry mustard. Stir in enough of the milk to make desired consistency. Set aside.

2. Lightly grease four cups of an egg poaching pan.* Place the poaching cups over pan of boiling water (water should not touch bottoms of cups); reduce heat to simmering. Break one egg into a measuring cup. Carefully slide egg into a poaching cup. Repeat with remaining eggs. Cover; cook for 6 to 8 minutes or until egg whites are completely set and yolks begin to thicken but are not hard. Run a knife around edges of cups to loosen eggs. Invert poaching cups to remove eggs.

3. Top bread slices with smoked salmon. Top with poached eggs. Top with mustard-sour cream mixture. If desired, sprinkle with sweet pepper. Season to taste with salt and black pepper.

Per serving: 206 cal., 10 g total fat (4 g sat. fat), 225 mg chol., 481 mg sodium, 14 g carb., 1 g fiber, 14 g pro.

*Test Kitchen Tip: If you don't have an egg poaching pan, lightly grease a 2-quart saucepan with cooking oil or shortening. Fill the pan halfway with water; bring to boiling. Reduce heat to simmering. Break one egg into a measuring cup. Carefully slide egg into water, holding the lip of the cup as close to the water as possible. Repeat with remaining eggs, spacing eggs equally. Simmer, uncovered, for 3 to 5 minutes or until egg whites are completely set and yolks begin to thicken but are not hard. Remove eggs with a slotted spoon.

Berry-Brie Quesadillas

Thanks to a creamy layer of Brie, this triple-berry pleaser is extra rich and extra satisfying.

Prep: 15 minutes   **Bake:** 8 minutes
Oven: 400°F
Makes 5 servings

5	7- to 8-inch flour tortillas
1	tablespoon butter, melted
4	ounces Brie cheese, cut into ¼-inch-thick slices (remove rind, if desired)
1	cup fresh blueberries
1	cup fresh raspberries
¼	cup honey
1	cup quartered fresh strawberries

1. Preheat oven to 400°F. For quesadillas, brush one side of each tortilla with melted butter. Place tortillas, buttered sides down, on a large baking sheet. Place Brie slices on one-half of each tortilla. Sprinkle blueberries over Brie. Fold other half of each tortilla over berries. Bake for 8 to 10 minutes or until golden brown and cheese is melted.

2. Meanwhile, for sauce: In a blender or food processor, combine the raspberries and honey. Cover and blend or process until smooth. Serve the quesadillas with the raspberry mixture and quartered strawberries.

Per serving: 269 cal., 11 g total fat (6 g sat. fat), 29 mg chol., 280 mg sodium, 37 g carb., 4 g fiber, 7 g pro.

Omelet Crepes

For a zesty topping, pass your favorite salsa.
Start to finish: 30 minutes
Makes 4 servings

  6   eggs
 ⅓   cup water
 ⅛   teaspoon salt
 ⅛   teaspoon ground black pepper
  2   tablespoons butter or margarine
  6   ounces smoked cooked ham, diced (about
        1¼ cups)
 ½   cup chopped green sweet pepper
 ¼   cup chopped onion
 ½   cup shredded cheddar cheese (2 ounces)
  8   6-inch purchased crepes

1. In a medium bowl, whisk together eggs, the water, salt, and black pepper. Set aside. In a large nonstick skillet, melt butter over medium heat. Add ham, sweet pepper, and onion; cook for 3 to 4 minutes or until vegetables are tender.

2. Pour egg mixture over ingredients in skillet. Cook over medium heat, without stirring, until mixture begins to set on the bottom and around edge. Using a large spatula, lift and fold partially cooked egg mixture so the uncooked portion flows underneath. Continue cooking and folding for 2 to 3 minutes or until egg mixture is cooked through but is still glossy and moist. Remove from heat immediately. Sprinkle with cheese. Cover and let stand about 2 minutes or until cheese melts.

3. In an 8-inch skillet, heat crepes, one at a time, over medium heat for a few seconds or until warm. Divide egg mixture into four portions. On each of four dinner plates, overlap two of the crepes, browned sides down. Spoon one portion of the egg mixture onto overlapped crepes on each plate. Roll crepes around egg mixture. Serve immediately.

Per serving: 587 cal., 36 g total fat (14 g sat. fat), 574 mg chol., 1,232 mg sodium, 32 g carb., 2 g fiber, 32 g pro.

Windowpane Eggs

Fresh sugar snap peas and grape tomatoes bring a garden-fresh note to these delicate eggs nestled in sourdough toast.
Start to finish: 20 minutes
Makes 2 servings

  3   to 4 teaspoons cooking oil
 ½   cup fresh sugar snap peas, strings and tips
        removed
 ½   cup grape tomatoes and/or yellow cherry
        tomatoes, halved
  2   teaspoons snipped fresh dill
        or ½ teaspoon dried dill
        Salt
        Freshly ground black pepper
  2   ½-inch-thick slices sourdough bread
        (approximately 5×4-inch rectangles)
  2   eggs

1. In a 12-inch skillet, heat 1 teaspoon of the oil over medium-low heat. Add sugar snap peas and tomatoes; cook and stir about 4 minutes or until the sugar snap peas are crisp-tender and tomatoes are heated through. Stir in dill. Season to taste with salt and pepper. Remove from the skillet. Cover and keep warm.

2. In the same skillet, heat another 1 teaspoon of the oil over medium heat. Brush both sides of each bread slice with the remaining oil. Cut or tear a hole in each slice of bread, leaving about ½ inch of bread around the perimeter. Place bread slices in hot skillet. Crack one egg into center of each bread slice. Sprinkle with salt and pepper. Cover and cook for 2 to 3 minutes. Using a wide spatula, turn bread over; cook about 2 minutes more or until eggs are desired doneness. Serve with sugar snap pea-tomato mixture.

Per serving: 236 cal., 13 g total fat (3 g sat. fat), 212 mg chol., 376 mg sodium, 20 g carb., 3 g fiber, 10 g pro.

All-Is-Calm Hot Chocolate

Keep the ready-to-use mix on hand so you can treat your family to this outrageously delicious sipper whenever you want.

Start to finish: 25 minutes
Oven: 350°F (to toast seeds)
Makes 12 servings total from the mix

> 8 **ounces semisweet or bittersweet chocolate chunks or pieces**
> ⅔ **cup sugar**
> ½ **cup unsweetened cocoa powder**
> ½ **teaspoon anise seeds, toasted* and crushed**
> ½ **teaspoon ground cinnamon**
> **Milk, half-and-half, or light cream**
> **Whipped cream (optional)**

1. For hot chocolate mix: In a large bowl, combine chocolate chunks or pieces, sugar, cocoa powder, toasted anise seeds, and cinnamon. Spoon into an airtight container, jar, or resealable plastic bag. Cover or seal.

2. For 4 servings of hot chocolate: In a medium saucepan, combine ⅔ cup of the hot chocolate mix and ¼ cup water; cook and stir over medium heat until chocolate is melted and mixture is smooth. Whisk in 4 cups milk, half-and-half, or light cream; heat through, whisking occasionally. Pour into mugs. If desired, top individual servings with whipped cream.

Per serving: 272 cal., 11 g total fat (6 g sat. fat), 18 mg chol., 122 mg sodium, 30 g carb., 3 g fiber, 9 g pro.

*Test Kitchen Tip: To toast anise seeds, preheat oven to 350°F. Place anise seeds in a shallow baking pan. Bake about 5 minutes or until toasted and aromatic, stirring once.

Green Onion Parker House Biscuits

side dishes

Choosing the right sides to complement a main dish can mean the difference between an ordinary meal and an exceptional one. These delectable and quick serve-along suggestions will help you add interest and lively flavor to just about any menu.

Green Onion Parker House Biscuits

Refrigerated biscuit dough and softened herb-blended cheese make these biscuits so quick to prepare, you can serve them even when your schedule is the most hectic.

Prep: 10 minutes   **Bake:** 8 minutes
Oven: 400°F
Makes 10 biscuits

1	**5.2-ounce container Boursin cheese with garlic and herb**
¼	**cup sliced green onions**
1	**12-ounce package (10) refrigerated biscuits**
1	**egg yolk**
1	**tablespoon water**
2	**tablespoons grated Parmesan cheese**
	Sliced green onions

1. Preheat oven to 400°F. In a small bowl, stir together Boursin cheese and the ¼ cup green onions. Set aside.

2. Unwrap biscuits. Using your fingers, gently split the biscuits horizontally. Place the biscuit bottoms on a greased cookie sheet. Spread about 1 tablespoon of the cheese mixture over *each* biscuit bottom. Replace biscuit tops.

3. In a small bowl, use a fork to beat together egg yolk and the water. Brush biscuit tops with egg yolk mixture. Sprinkle with Parmesan cheese and additional sliced green onions. Bake for 8 to 10 minutes or until golden brown. Serve warm.

Per biscuit: 149 cal., 8 g total fat (5 g sat. fat), 23 mg chol., 394 mg sodium, 16 g carb., 0 g fiber, 4 g pro.

Cheese-Garlic Crescents

Another time, try these full-flavored rolls with soft-style cream cheese with chive and onion in place of the semisoft cheese. Or for a party, make two batches, each with a different cheese.

Prep: 15 minutes **Bake**: 11 minutes
Oven: 375°F
Makes 8 crescents

- 1   **8-ounce package (8) refrigerated crescent rolls**
- ¼   **cup semisoft cheese with garlic and herb**
- 2   **tablespoons finely chopped walnuts, toasted**
   Nonstick cooking spray
   Milk
- 1   **tablespoon seasoned fine dry bread crumbs**

1. Preheat oven to 375°F. Unroll crescent rolls; divide into eight triangles. In a small bowl, stir together cheese and walnuts. Place a rounded measuring teaspoon of the cheese mixture near the center of the wide end of *each* crescent roll. Roll up crescent rolls, starting at the wide end.

2. Lightly coat a baking sheet with nonstick cooking spray. Place rolls, point sides down, on the prepared baking sheet. Brush tops lightly with milk; sprinkle with bread crumbs.

3. Bake about 11 minutes or until bottoms are browned. Serve warm.

Per crescent: 141 cal., 10 g total fat (3 g sat. fat), 6 mg chol., 254 mg sodium, 12 g carb., 0 g fiber, 3 g pro.

Cauliflower with Lemon Dressing

Serrano ham and manchego cheese are a seasoned ham and a sheep's-milk cheese imported from Spain. Look for them at food specialty shops.

Start to finish: 20 minutes
Makes 4 servings

- 2   **small heads cauliflower**
- ½   **cup water**
- 2   **to 3 ounces thinly sliced Serrano ham, prosciutto, or cooked ham**
- 1   **ounce manchego cheese or Monterey Jack cheese, thinly shaved**
- ¼   **cup olive oil or cooking oil**
- 2   **tablespoons lemon juice**
- ½   **teaspoon salt**
- ½   **teaspoon bottled minced garlic**
- ¼   **teaspoon sugar**
- ¼   **teaspoon dry mustard**
- ¼   **teaspoon freshly ground black pepper**
- 2   **tablespoons pine nuts, toasted**
- 2   **tablespoons capers, rinsed and drained**

1. Remove heavy leaves and tough stems from cauliflower; cut cauliflower into wedges. Place cauliflower wedges in a microwave-safe 3-quart casserole. Add the water. Microwave, covered, on 100% power (high) for 7 to 9 minutes or just until tender. Remove with a slotted spoon to serving plates. Top with ham and cheese.

2. Meanwhile, in a screw-top jar, combine oil, lemon juice, salt, garlic, sugar, mustard, and pepper. Cover and shake well to combine; drizzle over cauliflower. Sprinkle with pine nuts and capers.

Per serving: 207 cal., 18 g total fat (3 g sat. fat), 10 mg chol., 848 mg sodium, 7 g carb., 4 g fiber, 9 g pro.

Cauliflower goes from ordinary to company-special when it's drizzled with a lemon and garlic dressing and topped with spicy ham, cheese, capers, and **toasted pine nuts.**

Cauliflower with Lemon Dressing

Really Red Coleslaw

Really Red Coleslaw

Take a break from ordinary slaw with this impressively red fruity delight.

Start to finish: 15 minutes
Makes 8 servings

- 1   10-ounce package shredded red cabbage (about 6 cups)
- 1   medium red onion, slivered (1 cup)
- ½   cup dried tart red cherries
- ½   cup bottled red raspberry vinaigrette salad dressing
- 1   tablespoon seedless red raspberry preserves

1. In a large bowl, combine red cabbage, red onion, and dried cherries; set aside. In a small bowl, stir together vinaigrette and preserves; pour over cabbage mixture. Toss gently to coat.

Per serving: 108 cal., 6 g total fat (1 g sat. fat), 0 mg chol., 5 mg sodium, 12 g carb., 1 g fiber, 1 g pro.

Make-Ahead Directions: Prepare as directed. Cover and chill for up to 6 hours.

Barbecued Limas

A spunky barbecue sauce that starts with canned soup makes this old-fashioned bean-and-bacon combination a tasty reason to get out the can opener.

Start to finish: 25 minutes
Makes 6 servings

- 1   16-ounce package frozen baby lima beans
- 4   slices bacon, cut into ½-inch pieces
- ½   cup chopped onion
- 1   teaspoon bottled minced garlic
- 1   10¾-ounce can condensed tomato soup
- 2   tablespoons packed brown sugar
- 1   tablespoon white vinegar
- 1   tablespoon Worcestershire sauce
- 2   teaspoons yellow mustard
- 1   teaspoon chili powder

1. In a large saucepan, cook lima beans according to package directions; drain and set aside.

2. Meanwhile, in another large saucepan, cook bacon, onion, and garlic over medium heat until bacon is brown and onion is tender. Stir in tomato soup, brown sugar, vinegar, Worcestershire sauce, mustard, and chili powder. Bring to boiling; reduce heat. Cover and simmer for 5 minutes.

3. Stir cooked lima beans into tomato soup mixture; heat through.

Per serving: 195 cal., 3 g total fat (1 g sat. fat), 5 mg chol., 487 mg sodium, 34 g carb., 6 g fiber, 9 g pro.

Take It Along

When you need a potluck or picnic dish but have little time to cook, remember these two recipes. Both the coleslaw and the limas fill the bill—they cook quickly and are people pleasers. What's more, you can double either recipe if you're feeding a crowd.

Beet Greens with Walnuts and Blue Cheese

This delightfully sophisticated side dish **showcases beet greens** that are lightly cooked with walnuts and **sprinkled with blue cheese.**

Beet Greens with Walnuts and Blue Cheese

If you love beets, you'll enjoy equally tasty beet greens. When shopping for beet greens, look for deep green, fresh-looking leaves that are small to medium in size.

Start to finish: 15 minutes
Makes 4 servings

- 8 **ounces fresh beet greens**
- 2 **teaspoons cooking oil**
- 2 **tablespoons chopped walnuts**
- 1 **tablespoon crumbled blue cheese**
- ¼ **teaspoon ground black pepper**

1. Thoroughly clean beet greens. Drain well. Cut beet greens into 1-inch strips. In a large skillet, heat oil over medium-high heat. Add walnuts. Cook and stir for 2 minutes. Add beet greens. Cook and stir, uncovered, about 1 minute or just until wilted. Top individual servings with crumbled blue cheese and pepper.

Per serving: 55 cal., 5 g total fat (1 g sat. fat), 0 mg chol., 109 mg sodium, 3 g carb., 2 g fiber, 2 g pro.

Vary the Greens

Beet Greens with Walnuts and Blue Cheese also can be prepared with fresh spinach or Swiss chard. Whichever greens you choose, be sure to clean them thoroughly under cold running water to remove any dirt or sand. (It may take more than one rinsing.) Drain the greens very well before cutting them into strips.

Easy Parmesan Breadsticks

These versatile crispy, cheesy sticks can be served a couple of ways. Serve them restaurant-style as a meal starter. Or use them as a serve-along for soup or salad.

Prep: 15 minutes **Bake:** 10 minutes
Oven: 375°F
Makes 6 servings

- ½ **of a 12-ounce loaf baguette-style French bread (halve bread loaf crosswise)**
- **Nonstick cooking spray**
- ¼ **cup olive oil**
- 6 **tablespoons grated or finely shredded Parmesan cheese**
- **Purchased marinara sauce, warmed, and/or flavored oils (such as lemon-, basil-, or garlic-flavored)**

1. Preheat oven to 375°F. Cut bread lengthwise into quarters; cut into ¼- to ½-inch-wide strips. (Cut bread so there is crust on each strip.)

2. Line a 15×10×1-inch baking pan with foil; lightly coat foil with nonstick cooking spray. Arrange bread strips in a single layer; drizzle with oil. Using a spatula or tongs, carefully turn breadsticks to coat with oil. Sprinkle with Parmesan cheese.

3. Bake for 10 to 12 minutes or until browned and crisp. Serve with marinara sauce and/or flavored oils.

Per serving: 219 cal., 13 g total fat (3 g sat. fat), 4 mg chol., 539 mg sodium, 20 g carb., 2 g fiber, 5 g pro.

Dino Kale Sauté

If you enjoy kale in salads, you'll love this wilted greens side dish that's sprinkled with toasted bread crumbs, Worcestershire sauce, and a squeeze of lemon.

Start to finish: 15 minutes
Makes 4 servings

12	ounces dinosaur kale or regular kale, cut or torn into 1- to 2-inch pieces (about 12 cups)
2	tablespoons olive oil
¼	cup soft sourdough or French loaf bread crumbs
⅛	teaspoon ground black pepper
1	teaspoon Worcestershire sauce for chicken
	Lemon wedges (optional)

1. Rinse kale leaves thoroughly under cold running water. Drain well; set aside.

2. In a small skillet, heat 2 teaspoons of the oil over medium heat. Add bread crumbs; cook and stir for 1 to 2 minutes or until browned. Season with pepper; set aside.

3. In a large nonstick skillet, heat the remaining 4 teaspoons oil. Add kale; cover and cook for 1 minute. Uncover and cook and stir about 1 minute more or just until wilted.

4. Transfer kale to a serving dish. Drizzle with Worcestershire sauce. Sprinkle with the browned bread crumbs. If desired, squeeze lemon over all.
Per serving: 89 cal., 5 g total fat (1 g sat. fat), 0 mg chol., 53 mg sodium, 9 g carb., 4 g fiber, 2 g pro.

Lemon-Pepper Baby Broccoli

Baby broccoli, called Broccolini, is a cross between broccoli and Chinese kale. Because of its tender stem, it cooks quickly.

Start to finish: 20 minutes
Makes 8 servings

1	cup reduced-sodium chicken broth
1	tablespoon snipped fresh dill
2	teaspoons finely shredded lemon peel
1	teaspoon olive oil
½	teaspoon coarse salt
⅛	teaspoon crushed red pepper
⅛	teaspoon ground black pepper
1	pound baby broccoli or broccoli rabe
2	tablespoons butter
	Lemon halves or slices (optional)

1. In a large skillet, combine chicken broth, dill, lemon peel, olive oil, coarse salt, crushed red pepper, and black pepper. Bring to boiling; reduce heat. Cover and simmer for 5 minutes.

2. Add broccoli and butter to skillet. Cover and cook over medium heat for 6 to 8 minutes or until broccoli is tender. If desired, drain. Transfer broccoli mixture to a serving bowl. If desired, garnish with lemon halves or slices.
Per serving: 47 cal., 3 g total fat (2 g sat. fat), 8 mg chol., 489 mg sodium, 4 g carb., 2 g fiber, 2 g pro.

Fresh dill, shredded lemon peel, and
two types of pepper give tender baby broccoli
a zesty flavor boost. For extra tang, squirt on
some fresh lemon juice.

Lemon-Pepper Baby Broccoli

A creamy ginger-apricot dressing brings out the best in **summer-fresh chunks of honeydew melon,** rosy golden nectarine slices, and tangy apple pieces.

Honeydew and Nectarine Salad

Honeydew and Nectarine Salad

When summer fruits aren't in season, try this refreshing three-ingredient dressing on a combination of orange sections and banana slices.

Start to finish: 15 minutes
Makes 6 servings

½ of a medium honeydew melon, peeled, seeded, and cut into bite-size pieces (2 cups)

2 medium tart apples, cored, halved lengthwise, and cut into bite-size pieces

2 medium nectarines or peaches, pitted and thinly sliced

¼ cup vanilla low-fat yogurt

3 tablespoons apricot jam

¼ teaspoon ground ginger or ground nutmeg

1 cup fresh red raspberries

1. In a large bowl, combine melon, apples, and nectarines or peaches. For dressing: In a small bowl, stir together yogurt, jam, and ginger.

2. Spoon salad into salad dishes. Drizzle with dressing. Top with raspberries. Serve immediately.

Per serving: 109 cal., 1 g total fat (0 g sat. fat), 1 mg chol., 16 mg sodium, 27 g carb., 3 g fiber, 1 g pro.

Savory Couscous

Add a garden-fresh note to any meal by jazzing up couscous with mushrooms, carrot, green onions, and basil or thyme.

Start to finish: 20 minutes
Makes 8 servings

2 cups water

1½ cups sliced fresh mushrooms

½ cup shredded carrot

⅓ cup thinly sliced green onions

1 tablespoon butter or margarine

2 teaspoons instant chicken bouillon granules

½ teaspoon dried basil or thyme, crushed

1 10-ounce package quick-cooking couscous

1. In a medium saucepan, combine the water, mushrooms, carrot, green onions, butter, bouillon granules, and basil or thyme; bring to boiling. Stir in couscous. Remove from heat.

2. Cover; let stand about 5 minutes or until liquid is absorbed. Fluff with a fork before serving.

Per serving: 158 cal., 2 g total fat (1 g sat. fat), 4 mg chol., 241 mg sodium, 29 g carb., 2 g fiber, 5 g pro.

Orange Dream Fruit Salad

When you're too rushed to peel, seed, and chop fresh mango, look for jars of mango pieces in the refrigerator case of your supermarket's produce section.

Start to finish: 15 minutes
Makes 4 to 6 servings

1 cup chopped, peeled, seeded mango or papaya

1 11-ounce can mandarin orange sections, drained

1 cup seedless red and/or green grapes, halved

½ cup orange-flavored yogurt

¼ teaspoon poppy seeds

1. In a medium bowl, combine mango, drained mandarin oranges, and grapes. In a small bowl, stir together yogurt and poppy seeds. Gently stir yogurt mixture into the fruit mixture until combined.

Per serving: 136 cal., 1 g total fat (0 g sat. fat), 2 mg chol., 26 mg sodium, 32 g carb., 2 g fiber, 2 g pro.

Chipotle Coleslaw

Chipotle peppers are simply smoked jalapeño peppers. This recipe calls for ground chipotle chile pepper, which gives the coleslaw a spicy kick.

Start to finish: 20 minutes
Makes 6 servings

⅓ cup fat-free mayonnaise
1 tablespoon lime juice
2 teaspoons honey
¼ teaspoon ground cumin
⅛ to ¼ teaspoon ground chipotle chile pepper
3 cups shredded green cabbage
¾ cup whole kernel corn, thawed if frozen
¾ cup chopped red sweet pepper
⅓ cup thinly sliced red onion
⅓ cup chopped cilantro

1. In a small bowl, stir together mayonnaise, lime juice, honey, cumin, and chipotle chile pepper.

2. In a large bowl, combine cabbage, corn, sweet pepper, onion, and cilantro. Pour mayonnaise mixture over cabbage mixture. Toss lightly to coat. Serve immediately or cover and chill up to 24 hours.

Per serving: 55 cal., 0.7 g total fat (0 g sat. fat), 1.3 mg chol., 122 mg sodium, 13 g carbo., 2 g fiber, 2 g pro.

Asian Pea Pod Salad

Start to finish: 20 minutes
Makes 6 servings

6 cups torn romaine lettuce
2 cups fresh pea pods, trimmed and halved lengthwise
⅓ cup bottled Italian salad dressing
1 tablespoon hoisin sauce
1 tablespoon sesame seeds, toasted
4 radished, coarsely shredded

1. In a large salad bowl, toss together the lettuce and pea pods. In a small bowl, stir together the dressing and hoisin sauce. Pour over lettuce mixture and toss to coat. Sprinkle with sesame seeds and radish.

Per serving: 98 cal., 7 g total fat (1 g sat. fat), 0 mg chol., 153 mg sodium, 6 g carbo., 2 g fiber, 2 g pro.

This easy salad is packed with **garden freshness** and is not too spicy. Choose young **tender pea pods** that are moist to the touch, **bright green** in color, and filled end to end with peas.

Asian Pea Pod Salad

Greek Vegetable Salad

Greek Vegetable Salad

This healthful Greek-inspired salad of tomatoes, cucumber, sweet pepper, and feta cheese is lightly dressed in an herb vinaigrette.

Start to finish: 30 minutes
Makes 8 servings

2	cups chopped tomatoes
1	cup chopped cucumber
½	cup chopped yellow, red, or green sweet pepper
¼	cup chopped red onion
1½	teaspoons snipped fresh thyme or ½ teaspoon dried thyme, crushed
1	teaspoon snipped fresh oregano or ¼ teaspoon dried oregano, crushed
2	tablespoons white balsamic vinegar or regular balsamic vinegar
2	tablespoons olive oil
	Leaf lettuce (optional)
½	cup crumbled feta cheese (2 ounces)

1. In a large bowl, combine tomatoes, cucumber, sweet pepper, red onion, thyme, and oregano. For dressing, in a small bowl, whisk together balsamic vinegar and olive oil. Pour dressing over vegetable mixture. Toss gently to coat.

2. If desired, line a serving bowl with lettuce; spoon in vegetable mixture. Sprinkle with feta cheese.

Per serving: 65 cal., 5 g total fat (1 g sat. fat), 3 mg chol., 120 mg sodium, 4 g carbo., 1 g fiber, 2 g pro.

Soft Pretzels

Serve these versatile breads as a snack or as a serve-along for soup or salad.

Prep: 15 minutes **Bake:** 12 minutes **Oven:** 375F°F
Makes 8 pretzels

1	package (8) refrigerated breadsticks
1	egg white
1	tablespoon water
	Sesame seeds or poppy seeds

1. Preheat oven to 375°F. Lightly grease a baking sheet; set aside. Unroll breadsticks so the dough lays flat. Gently pull each breadstick into a 16-inch-long rope. Shape each rope into a pretzel by crossing one end over the other to form a circle, overlapping about 4 inches from each end. Take one end of the rope in each hand and twist once at the point where the rope overlaps. Carefully lift each end across to the opposite edge of the circle; tuck ends under edges to make pretzel shape. Moisten the ends; press to seal. Place pretzels on prepared baking sheet.

2. In a small bowl, beat egg white and the water with a fork until well mixed. Brush pretzels with egg white mixture. Sprinkle with sesame seeds and/or poppy seeds. Bake for 12 to 15 minutes or until golden brown.

Per pretzel: 114 cal., 3 g total fat (1 g sat. fat), 0 mg chol., 297 mg sodium, 18 g carbo., 1 g fiber, 4 g pro.

Great Greek Green Beans

Tomatoes, olives, oregano, and feta cheese lend the Greek notes to this zesty side dish. Serve it with grilled or broiled chicken breasts or lamb chops.

Prep: 10 minutes **Cook:** 20 minutes
Makes 6 servings

½ cup chopped onion
1 clove garlic, minced
2 tablespoons olive oil
1 28-ounce can diced tomatoes, undrained
¼ cup sliced pitted ripe olives
1 teaspoon dried oregano, crushed
2 9-ounce packages or one 16-ounce
    package frozen French-cut green beans,
    thawed and drained
½ cup crumbled feta cheese (2 ounces)

1. In a large skillet, cook onion and garlic in hot oil about 5 minutes or until tender. Add undrained tomatoes, olives, and oregano. Bring to boiling; reduce heat. Boil gently, uncovered, for 10 minutes. Add beans. Return to boiling. Boil gently, uncovered, about 8 minutes or until desired consistency and beans are tender.

2. Transfer to a serving bowl; sprinkle with cheese. If desired, serve with a slotted spoon.
Per serving: 132 cal., 7 g total fat (2 g sat. fat), 8 mg chol., 419 mg sodium, 15 g carbo., 5 g fiber, 4 g pro.

Bow Ties with Mushrooms and Spinach

This mushroom, vegetable, and pasta combo makes a savory side dish that takes almost no time. Remember this recipe next time you need a great side dish for grilled or roasted meat.

Prep: 10 minutes **Cook:** 10 minutes
Makes 4 servings

6 ounces dried farfalle (bow tie pasta)
1 medium onion, chopped (½ cup)
1 cup sliced portobello or other fresh
    mushrooms
1 tablespoon olive oil
2 cloves garlic, minced
4 cups thinly sliced fresh spinach
1 teaspoon snipped fresh thyme
⅛ teaspoon pepper
2 tablespoons shredded Parmesan cheese

1. Cook farfalle according to package directions. Drain well.

2. Meanwhile, in a large skillet, cook and stir onion, mushrooms, and garlic in hot oil over medium heat for 2 to 3 minutes or until mushrooms are nearly tender. Stir in spinach, thyme, and pepper; cook for 1 minute or until heated through and spinach is slightly wilted. Stir in cooked pasta; toss gently to mix. Sprinkle with cheese.
Per serving: 219 cal., 5 g total fat (1 g sat. fat), 2 mg chol., 86 mg sodium, 35 g carbo., 4 g fiber, 9 g pro.

Bow Ties with Mushrooms and Spinach

Wasabi Party Mix

snacks & desserts

Taking time to make treats such as snacks and desserts may seem like a luxury that's hard to squeeze into your schedule. But with these incredible time-saving recipes, you can make sweets and savory tidbits almost any time.

Wasabi Party Mix

As a treat for guests who drop by unexpectedly, keep some of this packs-a-punch snack mix on hand—you can store it in the freezer for up to 4 months.

Start to finish: 10 minutes
Makes 20 cups

5 **cups wasabi-flavored dehydrated peas***
4 **cups bite-size toasted rice cracker mix**
4 **cups sesame sticks**
4 **cups honey-roasted peanuts**
2 **cups shredded coconut**

1. In a very large bowl, combine peas, rice cracker mix, sesame sticks, peanuts, and coconut.

Per ¼ cup: 99 cal., 6 g total fat (2 g sat. fat), 0 mg chol., 134 mg sodium, 9 g carb., 1 g fiber, 3 g pro.

*Test Kitchen Tip: If you can't find wasabi-flavored dehydrated peas at your supermarket, make your own. Place 5 cups dehydrated peas in a large bowl. Lightly coat peas with nonstick cooking spray, tossing to coat evenly. Sprinkle with 2 to 3 teaspoons wasabi powder; toss to coat.

Zesty Smoked Trout Spread

If you have leftover spread, slather some on a bagel for a quick lunch.

Start to finish: 15 minutes
Makes 1¾ cups

8	ounces smoked trout fillets (or other smoked white fish), skin and bones removed and flaked
2	3-ounce packages cream cheese, softened
¼	cup dairy sour cream
3	tablespoons finely chopped shallot or onion
1½	teaspoons finely shredded lemon peel
3	tablespoons lemon juice
¼	teaspoon freshly ground black pepper
	Fresh chives or chopped green onion (optional)
3	red sweet peppers, seeded and cut into 1-inch-wide strips
	Assorted crackers or flatbreads

1. In a medium bowl, stir together smoked trout, cream cheese, sour cream, shallot, lemon peel, lemon juice, and pepper until well mixed, smearing the trout against the side of the bowl with the back of the spoon while stirring.

2. Transfer spread to a small serving bowl. If desired, top with chives or green onion. Serve with sweet pepper strips and crackers or flatbreads.

Per 2 tablespoons spread: 75 cal., 5 g total fat (3 g sat. fat), 29 mg chol., 84 mg sodium, 4 g carb., 0 g fiber, 3 g pro.

Honey-Nut Spread

Serve this creamy spread with your choice of graham crackers or sliced fruit.

Start to finish: 10 minutes
Makes about ⅔ cup spread

- ⅓ cup reduced-fat cream cheese (Neufchâtel) (about 3 ounces), softened
- 1 tablespoon honey
- 1 tablespoon chopped walnuts
- ⅛ teaspoon ground cinnamon or ground cardamom
- 2 tablespoons snipped dried figs, dates, or dried apricots
- Milk (optional)
- Graham crackers, apple slices, or pear slices

1. In a small bowl, stir together cream cheese, honey, walnuts, and cinnamon; stir in dried fruit.

2. If necessary, stir in 2 to 3 teaspoons milk to make desired spreading consistency. Serve with graham crackers or fruit.

Per 1 tablespoon spread with 2 graham cracker squares:
99 cal., 4 g total fat (2 g sat. fat), 6 mg chol., 119 mg sodium, 14 g carb., 1 g fiber, 2 g pro.

Warm Artichoke and Salsa Dip

Suit your taste by selecting a green salsa with a heat level that you like.

Start to finish: 15 minutes
Makes 1½ cups

- 1 12-ounce jar or two 6-ounce jars marinated artichoke hearts
- ⅓ cup sliced green onions
- 2 tablespoons bottled green salsa
- ½ cup shredded Monterey Jack or white cheddar cheese (2 ounces)
- ¼ cup dairy sour cream
- ¼ cup snipped fresh cilantro
- Toasted baguette slices and/or assorted crackers

1. Drain artichokes, discarding marinade. Coarsely chop artichokes. In a small saucepan, combine chopped artichokes, green onions, and salsa. Cook over medium heat until heated through, stirring frequently. Remove from heat. Stir in cheese, sour cream, and cilantro. Serve immediately with toasted baguette slices and/or assorted crackers.

Per ¼ cup dip: 144 cal., 13 g total fat (5 g sat. fat), 12 mg chol., 256 mg sodium, 5 g carb., 0 g fiber, 3 g pro.

Banana-Split Snack Mix

The goodies—toasted nuts, dried fruits, and chocolate pieces—tend to sink to the bottom, so be sure to stir the mix before serving.

Start to finish: 15 minutes
Makes about 14 cups

11 cups popped popcorn or one 3-ounce
       package microwave popcorn
    Nonstick cooking spray
 2 teaspoons sugar
 1 teaspoon ground cinnamon
 2 cups dried banana chips
 1 cup dried cherries or raisins
 1 cup miniature semisweet chocolate kisses
       or semisweet chocolate pieces
 1 cup pecan halves or pieces, toasted

1. If using microwave popcorn, pop corn according to package directions. Pour popped corn into a very large bowl. Remove any unpopped kernels from popped corn. Coat popcorn lightly with nonstick cooking spray. Toss popcorn and coat again with nonstick cooking spray. Repeat twice more.

2. In a small bowl, combine sugar and cinnamon; sprinkle over warm popcorn and toss lightly to coat. Stir in banana chips, dried cherries, semisweet chocolate kisses, and pecans. Store in an airtight container for up to 1 week.

Per 1 cup: 215 cal., 12 g total fat (5 g sat. fat), 1 mg chol., 8 mg sodium, 26 g carb., 3 g fiber, 3 g pro.

Oven Toasting Nuts

Using toasted nuts for Banana-Split Snack Mix gives it a richer, nuttier flavor. To toast nuts, arrange them in a single layer in a shallow baking pan. Bake them in a 350°F oven for 5 to 10 minutes or until light golden brown. Watch carefully and stir once or twice so the nuts don't burn.

Rosemary-Seasoned Nuts

Satisfy a snack attack with a handful of these savory nibbles. They're terrific made with just one nut or a blend of all three.

Prep: 10 minutes **Bake:** 15 minutes
Oven: 350°F
Makes about 3 cups

    Nonstick cooking spray
 1 egg white
 2 teaspoons snipped fresh rosemary
       or 1 teaspoon dried rosemary, crushed
½ teaspoon salt
½ teaspoon coarsely ground black pepper
 3 cups walnuts, hazelnuts (filberts), and/or
       whole almonds
    Fresh rosemary sprigs (optional)

1. Preheat oven to 350°F. Line a 13×9×2-inch baking pan with foil; lightly coat foil with nonstick cooking spray and set aside. In a medium bowl, beat egg white with a fork until frothy. Add snipped or dried rosemary, salt, and pepper, beating with the fork until combined. Add nuts; toss to coat.

2. Spread nut mixture in an even layer in the prepared pan. Bake for 15 to 20 minutes or until golden brown, stirring once.

3. Remove foil with nuts from pan; set aside to cool. Break up any large pieces. If desired, garnish with rosemary sprigs.

Per ¼ cup: 198 cal., 20 g total fat (2 g sat. fat), 0 mg chol., 102 mg sodium, 4 g carb., 2 g fiber, 5 g pro.

Rosemary-Seasoned Nuts

For a party, **scoop these herb-coated nuts into simple paper cones.** This way each person can munch from a cone while **mingling with the other guests.**

Caramel Clementines

Clementines, tangerines, satsuma oranges, and dancy oranges are all types of mandarin oranges and can be used interchangeably in this recipe. Typically, tangerines and dancy oranges have more seeds.

Prep: 15 minutes   **Cook:** 15 minutes
Makes 6 servings

- 6   clementines or other tangerine variety
- 1   14½-ounce can apricot nectar (1¾ cups)
- ½   cup sugar
    Dash cayenne pepper (optional)
- 2   tablespoons Southern Comfort, orange
    liqueur, or orange juice
    Pomegranate seeds (optional)

1. Peel clementines and remove any of the fibrous strands on the fruit. Place whole clementines in a medium saucepan; add apricot nectar, sugar, and, if desired, cayenne pepper. Bring to boiling; reduce heat. Cover and simmer for 5 minutes. Using a slotted spoon, transfer clementines to six dessert dishes. Continue to gently boil apricot nectar mixture about 15 minutes or until thick and syrupy. Remove from heat.

2. Stir Southern Comfort, orange liqueur, or orange juice into syrupy mixture. Spoon over clementines. If desired, sprinkle individual servings with a few pomegranate seeds. Serve warm.

Per serving: 151 cal., 0 g total fat, 0 mg chol., 3 mg sodium, 36 g carb., 2 g fiber, 1 g pro.

Fill-the-Grill Nectarine Toss

When it comes to enjoying fresh summer fruits, there's nothing better than these succulent, cinnamon-grilled nectarines served over big bowls of ice cream.

Prep: 15 minutes   **Grill:** 8 minutes
Makes 6 servings

- 6   medium nectarines, halved and pitted
- 2   tablespoons olive oil
    Ground cinnamon or nutmeg
- 3   cups vanilla ice cream
    Coarsely chopped chocolate chunks

1. Place a grill wok or grill basket on the rack of an uncovered grill directly over medium coals; heat for 5 minutes. Meanwhile, brush nectarines with olive oil. Sprinkle with cinnamon. Place nectarine halves in the preheated grill wok or basket. Grill for 8 to 10 minutes or until heated through, turning gently halfway through grilling.

2. To serve, divide ice cream among six dessert bowls. Top ice cream with grilled nectarines. Sprinkle with chocolate chunks. Serve immediately.

Per serving: 312 cal., 19 g total fat (9 g sat. fat), 46 mg chol., 46 mg sodium, 36 g carb., 2 g fiber, 4 g pro.

Fill-the-Grill Nectarine Toss

Fluffy Cranberry Mousse

Fluffy Cranberry Mousse

During the winter, serve this festive dessert as the luscious ending to a special meal. In summer, beat the heat with the same mixture spooned into small dessert dishes and frozen.

Start to finish: 20 minutes
Makes 12 servings

- ½ of an 8-ounce package cream cheese, softened
- 2 tablespoons sugar
- ½ teaspoon vanilla
- ½ cup frozen cranberry juice concentrate, thawed
- 1 16-ounce can whole cranberry sauce
- 1½ cups whipping cream
  Sweetened Cranberries (optional)

1. In a large bowl, beat cream cheese with an electric mixer on medium speed for 30 seconds. Beat in sugar and vanilla until smooth. Slowly add cranberry concentrate, beating until very smooth. In a small bowl, stir the whole cranberry sauce to remove any large lumps; set aside.

2. In a chilled large bowl, beat whipping cream with an electric mixer on low to medium speed until soft peaks form (tips curl). Fold about half of the cranberry sauce and half of the whipped cream into the cream cheese mixture. Fold in the remaining cranberry sauce and whipped cream.

3. Spoon cranberry mixture into 12 chilled small dessert dishes or a large serving bowl. If desired, spoon Sweetened Cranberries on top.

Per serving: 223 cal., 14 g total fat (9 g sat. fat), 51 mg chol., 45 mg sodium, 23 g carb., 1 g fiber, 1 g pro.

Sweetened Cranberries: In a medium skillet, combine 1 cup fresh cranberries, ⅓ cup sugar, and 2 tablespoons water. Cook and stir over medium heat until sugar dissolves and cranberries just begin to pop. Remove from heat. Cover and chill until serving time.

Make-Ahead Directions: Prepare as directed through Step 2. Cover and chill for up to 24 hours. (Or spoon cranberry mixture into 12 small freezer-safe dessert dishes. Cover and freeze for up to 24 hours. To serve, uncover and let stand for 1 to 2 minutes to soften slightly.) If desired, top individual servings with Sweetened Cranberries.

Chocolate–Butter Mint Fondue

If you like the combination of salty and sweet, try chunky pretzels for dipping.
Start to finish: 20 minutes
Makes 6 to 8 servings

- 1 14-ounce can sweetened condensed milk
- 1 7-ounce jar marshmallow creme
- 1 6-ounce package semisweet chocolate pieces
- ⅓ cup crushed butter mints
- ¼ cup milk
- 2 tablespoons crème de cacao (optional)
  Strawberries, pineapple chunks, cubed pound cake, and/or cubed angel food cake

1. In a medium saucepan, combine sweetened condensed milk, marshmallow creme, chocolate pieces, and butter mints. Cook and stir over low heat until chocolate melts. Stir in milk and, if desired, crème de cacao.

2. Transfer to a fondue pot; place over fondue burner. Spear strawberries, pineapple, pound cake, and/or angel food cake with fondue forks; dip into fondue mixture, swirling to coat.

Per serving: 665 cal., 22 g total fat (13 g sat. fat), 106 mg chol., 271 mg sodium, 114 g carb., 3 g fiber, 10 g pro.

Lemon Cheesecake Mousse

For a fancy presentation, layer the mousse with crushed gingersnaps in pretty parfait glasses.

Start to finish: 10 minutes
Makes 6 servings

1   8-ounce package cream cheese, softened
½   cup frozen lemonade concentrate, thawed
½   teaspoon vanilla
1   8-ounce container frozen whipped dessert topping, thawed
    Purchased gingersnaps (optional)

1. In a medium bowl, beat the cream cheese with an electric mixer on medium to high speed for 30 seconds. Beat in lemonade concentrate and vanilla. Fold in whipped topping. Divide among six dessert dishes. If desired, serve with gingersnaps.
Per serving: 282 cal., 20 g total fat (15 g sat. fat), 42 mg chol., 113 mg sodium, 21 g carb., 0 g fiber, 3 g pro.

Chocolate-Mint Sandwich Cookies

Three chocolate-flavored ingredients add up to a chocolate lover's delight.

Start to finish: 15 minutes
Makes 4 sandwich cookies

⅓   cup canned whipped chocolate or vanilla frosting
8   layered chocolate-mint candies, chopped
8   purchased soft chocolate cookies

1. In a small bowl, stir together frosting and chopped candies. Spread frosting mixture on the flat side of each of half of the cookies. Top with the remaining cookies, flat sides down.
Per sandwich cookie: 420 cal., 23 g total fat (11 g sat. fat), 1 mg chol., 195 mg sodium, 56 g carb., 2 g fiber, 3 g pro.

Chocolate–Peanut Butter Sandwich Cookies: Prepare as directed, except omit chocolate-mint candies and stir 2 tablespoons creamy peanut butter into frosting. Stir ¼ cup chopped cocktail peanuts or chocolate-covered peanuts into frosting mixture.
Per sandwich cookie: 468 cal., 28 g total fat (11 g sat. fat), 0 mg chol., 258 mg sodium, 53 g carb., 3 g fiber, 7 g pro.

Apricot-Peach Cobbler

Biscuit mix is the key to this sunny cobbler that is ready in only minutes. Chances are it will take less time than that for your family to eat it up.

Prep: 10 minutes   **Bake:** per package directions
Makes 6 servings

1   15-ounce can unpeeled apricot halves in light syrup
1   7.75-ounce packet cinnamon swirl biscuit mix (Bisquick® complete)
1   21-ounce can peach pie filling
1   teaspoon vanilla
    Vanilla ice cream (optional)

1. Preheat oven to temperature called for on biscuit mix package. Drain apricot halves, reserving syrup. Prepare biscuit mix according to package directions, except use ½ cup of the reserved apricot syrup in place of the water called for on the package. Bake according to package directions.

2. Meanwhile, in a medium saucepan, combine peach pie filling, drained apricots, and any remaining apricot syrup. Heat through. Remove from heat; stir in vanilla. Spoon fruit mixture into bowls. Top with the warm biscuits. If desired, serve with vanilla ice cream.
Per serving: 284 cal., 4 g total fat (0 g sat. fat), 0 mg chol., 346 mg sodium, 59 g carb., 2 g fiber, 3 g pro.

Hot Taffy Apple Pita Pizza

If caramel apples are a favorite, you won't be able to pass up this creative variation of the fruit treat-on-a-stick.

Prep: 15 minutes **Bake**: 10 minutes
Oven: 400°F
Makes 8 servings

- 2   pita bread rounds
- ½   cup purchased caramel dip for apples
- ¼   cup dairy sour cream
- 1   20-ounce can sliced apples, well drained
- 1   tablespoon butter, melted
- 2   tablespoons sugar
- ¼   teaspoon ground cinnamon
- ⅓   cup chopped pecans
     Vanilla or cinnamon ice cream (optional)

1. Preheat oven to 400°F. Place pita bread rounds on an ungreased baking sheet. In a small bowl, combine ¼ cup of the caramel dip and the sour cream; spread over pitas. Top with drained apples. Drizzle with melted butter. In a small bowl, combine sugar and cinnamon; sprinkle over apples. Drizzle with the remaining ¼ cup caramel dip;* sprinkle with pecans.

2. Bake about 10 minutes or until heated through. Serve warm. If desired, serve with ice cream.

Per serving: 233 cal., 10 g total fat (3 g sat. fat), 9 mg chol., 142 mg sodium, 36 g carb., 2 g fiber, 3 g pro.

*Test Kitchen Tip: If the caramel dip is too thick to drizzle, heat it in a saucepan or the microwave just until it thins slightly. An easy way to drizzle the dip is to spoon it into a plastic bag, snip off one corner, and squeeze the bag.

Caramel Apple Pastry

Refrigerated piecrust is a dessert lover's best friend. It's versatile, convenient, and—best of all—tastes wonderful, especially when paired with sliced apples and brown sugar.

Prep: 10 minutes **Bake**: 15 minutes
Cool: 5 minutes
Oven: 450°F
Makes 6 servings

- ½   of a 15-ounce package (1 crust) rolled refrigerated unbaked piecrust
- 1   tablespoon butter
- 2   20-ounce cans sliced apples, well drained
- ½   cup packed brown sugar
- 1   tablespoon lemon juice
- 1   teaspoon apple pie spice or ground cinnamon
- 1   tablespoon purchased cinnamon-sugar
     Cinnamon or vanilla ice cream (optional)
     Caramel ice cream topping (optional)

1. Preheat oven to 450°F. Bring piecrust to room temperature in microwave oven according to package directions; set aside. In a large ovenproof skillet, melt butter over high heat; stir in drained apple slices, brown sugar, lemon juice, and apple pie spice. Spread evenly in skillet. Cook until bubbly.

2. Meanwhile, on a lightly floured surface, unroll piecrust. Sprinkle piecrust with cinnamon-sugar; rub into crust with your fingers. Carefully place piecrust, cinnamon-sugar side up, over bubbly apple mixture in skillet. Tuck in piecrust around edge of skillet, using a spatula to press edge down slightly.

3. Bake about 15 minutes or until piecrust is golden brown. Cool for 5 minutes. Carefully invert skillet onto a serving platter; remove skillet. Serve warm. If desired, serve with ice cream and caramel topping.

Per serving: 381 cal., 12 g total fat (5 g sat. fat), 12 mg chol., 159 mg sodium, 69 g carb., 3 g fiber, 1 g pro.

Fruity Waffle Bowls

Waffle cone bowls are sized just right to hold a fruit and pudding dessert. Another time fill them with your favorite ice cream and toppers.

Start to finish: 15 minutes
Makes 4 servings

1	4-serving-size package instant lemon or white chocolate pudding mix
1⅓	cups fat-free milk
1	cup fresh fruit (such as blueberries, sliced kiwifruit, sliced strawberries, sliced bananas, or raspberries)
4	waffle ice cream bowls or large waffle ice cream cones
	Fresh mint leaves (optional)

1. Prepare pudding according to package directions, except use the 1⅓ cups milk. Spoon fruit into waffle bowls or cones. Top with pudding. If desired, garnish with fresh mint. Serve immediately.

Per serving: 196 cal., 3 g total fat (1 g sat. fat), 6 mg chol., 399 mg sodium, 40 g carbo., 1 g fiber, 3 g pro.

Baked Fruit Ambrosia

Spoon frozen yogurt or vanilla ice cream over this cinnamon-spiced fruit compote.

Prep: 10 minutes **Bake:** 15 minutes
Oven: 350°F
Makes 4 servings

- 2 **medium oranges**
- 1 **8-ounce can pineapple tidbits (juice pack), drained**
- ¼ **teaspoon ground cinnamon**
- 2 **tablespoons shredded coconut**
  Fresh raspberries (optional)

1. Finely shred ½ teaspoon peel from one of the oranges; set peel aside. Peel and section oranges. Cut orange sections into bite-size pieces. Divide orange pieces and pineapple among four 6-ounce custard cups. Sprinkle with orange peel and cinnamon. Top with coconut.

2. Bake in a 350°F oven about 15 minutes or until fruit is heated through and coconut is golden brown. If desired, garnish with fresh raspberries. Serve warm.

Per serving: 66 cal., 1 g total fat (1 g sat. fat), 0 mg chol., 12 mg sodium, 14 g carbo., 2 g fiber, 1 g pro.

Rocky Road Parfaits

This two-tone pudding dessert iss topped with a rocky road trio of peanuts, marshmallows, and chocolate.

Prep: 15 minutes **Stand:** 5 minutes
Makes 4 servings

- 1 **4-serving-size package chocolate or chocolate fudge instant pudding mix**
- 2 **cups milk**
- ½ **cup frozen whipped dessert topping, thawed**
- ¼ **cup unsalted peanuts, coarsely chopped**
- ¼ **cup tiny marshmallows**
  Chocolate curls (optional)

1. Prepare pudding mix according to package directions using the milk. Remove ¾ cup of the pudding and place in a small bowl; fold in whipped topping until combined.

2. Divide the remaining chocolate pudding among four 6-ounce glasses or dessert dishes. Top with dessert topping mixture. Let stand for 5 to 10 minutes or until set.

3. Sprinkle with peanuts, marshmallows, and, if desired, chocolate curls just before serving.

Per serving: 246 cal., 9 g total fat (4 g sat. fat), 10 mg chol., 412 mg sodium, 34 g carbo., 1 g fiber, 7 g pro.

Make-Ahead Directions: Make and chill this pudding dessert the day before, then sprinkle with nuts and marshmallows just before serving.

Warm Chocolate Bread Pudding

Here's a quick and easy way to use up leftover French or Italian bread and transform it into a rich-tasting satisfying chocolate dessert.

Prep: 15 minutes **Bake:** 15 minutes
Oven: 350°F
Makes 4 servings

   Nonstick cooking spray
2 cups firm-textured white bread cubes
⅔ cup milk
¼ cup granulated sugar
¼ cup miniature semisweet chocolate pieces
3 eggs
1 teaspoon finely shredded orange peel or tangerine peel
½ teaspoon vanilla
   Powdered sugar or frozen whipped dessert topping (optional)

1. Preheat oven to 350°F. Lightly coat four ¾-cup soufflé dishes or 6-ounce custard cups with cooking spray. Place the bread cubes in the souffl dishes.

2. In a small saucepan combine milk, granulated sugar, and chocolate. Cook and stir over low heat until chocolate is melted; remove from heat. If necessary, beat with a wire whisk until smooth.

3. In a small bowl lightly beat eggs; gradually stir in the chocolate mixture. Stir in orange peel and vanilla. Pour egg mixture over bread cubes; press bread with the back of a spoon to be sure it is all moistened.

4. Bake in the preheated oven for 15 to 20 minutes or until tops appear firm and a knife inserted near the centers comes out clean. Cool slightly on a wire rack. If desired, sprinkle with powdered sugar or top with whipped topping.

Per serving: 170 cal., 4 g total fat (2 g sat. fat), 1 mg chol., 143 mg sodium, 26 g carbo., 2 g fiber, 5 g pro.

Fresh Strawberry Fool

Fresh berries and a luscious yogurt-whipped cream make a simple, yet elegant classic English dessert. Crumbled cookies add delightful crunch.

Start to finish: 15 minutes
Makes 4 servings

½ cup whipping cream
⅓ cup powdered sugar
½ teaspoon vanilla
1 8-ounce carton low-fat lemon yogurt
3 cups sliced fresh strawberries or 2 cups fresh blueberries
½ cup coarsely crumbled shortbread cookies (5 cookies)

1. In a chilled medium bowl combine whipping cream, powdered sugar, and vanilla. Beat with chilled beaters of an electric mixer on medium speed or a chilled rotary beater until soft peaks form (tips curl). By hand, fold in the yogurt.

2. Spoon the whipped cream mixture into four dessert dishes. Top with berries. Sprinkle with the crumbled cookies.

Per serving: 272 cal., 15 g total fat (8 g sat. fat), 47 mg chol., 98 mg sodium, 32 g carbo., 3 g fiber, 4 g pro.

Make-Ahead Directions: Prepare as directed, except do not sprinkle with crumbled cookies. Cover and chill for up to 2 hours. To serve, sprinkle with crumbled cookies.

Fresh Strawberry Fool

Raspberry Cheesecake Shakes

Craving the **richness of cheesecake** but don't have the time to bake one? Experience a glass of **cheesecake heaven.**

Raspberry Cheesecake Shakes

Start to finish: 10 minutes
Makes 6 servings

1   12-ounce package frozen unsweetened red raspberries, thawed
1   3-ounce package cream cheese, softened
¼   teaspoon almond extract
1   quart vanilla ice cream, softened
2   12-ounce cans or bottles cream soda
    Fresh raspberries (optional)

1. In a blender, combine raspberries, cream cheese, and almond extract; add half of the ice cream and ½ cup of the cream soda. Cover and blend until smooth.

2. Pour into six 16-ounce glasses. Add a scoop of the remaining ice cream to each glass. Top with remaining cream soda.

3. If desired, garnish with fresh raspberries. Serve immediately.

Per serving: 305 cal., 15 g total fat (9 g sat. fat), 54 mg chol., 130 mg sodium, 36 g carbo., 2 g fiber, 4 g pro.

Ultimate Chocolate Sundaes

If you prefer less-sweet, darker chocolate, use bittersweet chocolate in this recipe.
Start to finish: 30 minutes
Makes 8 servings

8   ounces semisweet or bittersweet chocolate, coarsely chopped
⅓   cup water
¼   cup granulated sugar
¼   cup pear liqueur or pear nectar
4   small Forelle or Bosc pears (1 pound total)
3   tablespoons butter
2   tablespoons granulated sugar
1   quart vanilla ice cream

1. For chocolate sauce, in a small saucepan, combine chocolate, water, and the 14 cup sugar. Melt chocolate over low heat, stirring slowly and constantly. Stir in pear liqueur. Set aside to cool slightly.

2. Peel pears, if desired; cut into halves and remove cores.* Leave stem on one portion, if desired. In a large skillet, melt butter. Add pear halves; cook over medium heat about 12 minutes or until brown and tender, turning once. Add the 2 tablespoons sugar. Cook and stir gently until sugar is dissolved and pears are glazed.

3. To assemble, place scoops of ice cream in 8 dessert bowls. Spoon a pear half and some butter mixture around the ice cream in each bowl. Top with the chocolate sauce.

Per serving: 538 cal., 33 g total fat (20 g sat. fat), 132 mg chol., 119 mg sodium, 56 g carbo., 3 g fiber, 7 g pro.

*Test Kitchen Tip: If pears are larger cut into sixths or eighths (should have about 16 pieces).

Bakery-fresh brownies—milk chocolate, blond, or marbled—are the **secret shortcut** to creating this **dazzling** 15-minute dessert.

A Billow of Berries `n´ Brownies

A Billow of Berries `n´ Brownies

Start to finish: 15 minutes
Makes 12 servings

- 4 cups fresh red raspberries
- 4 to 5 tablespoons sugar
- 2 teaspoons finely shredded orange peel
- 2 cups whipping cream
- ¼ cup raspberry liqueur (Chambord) (optional)
- 4 3-inch squares purchased unfrosted brownies (such as milk chocolate, blond, or marbled brownies), cut into irregular chunks

1. Set aside 8 to 10 of the raspberries. In a medium bowl, combine the remaining berries, the sugar, and orange peel. Spoon berry mixture into a 1- to 1½-quart compote dish or serving bowl.

2. In a chilled bowl, combine whipping cream and, liqueur (if desired). Beat with chilled beaters of an electric mixer on medium speed until soft peaks form (tips curl). Spoon on top of raspberry mixture. Top whipped cream with brownie chunks and the reserved raspberries.

Per serving: 263 cal., 19 g total fat (10 g sat. fat), 69 mg chol., 63 mg sodium, 23 g carbo., 5 g fiber, 3 g pro.

Double Chocolate Brownies

For a triple dose of chocolate, serve this decadent brownie with vanilla or peppermint ice cream and hot fudge topping.

Prep: 10 minutes **Bake:** 15 minutes
Oven: 350°F
Makes 16 brownies

- Nonstick cooking spray
- ¼ cup butter or margarine
- ⅔ cup granulated sugar
- ½ cup cold water
- 1 teaspoon vanilla
- 1 cup all-purpose flour
- ¼ cup unsweetened cocoa powder
- 1 teaspoon baking powder
- ¼ cup miniature semisweet chocolate pieces
- 2 teaspoons sifted powdered sugar

1. Preheat oven to 350°F. Lightly coat the bottom of a 9x9x2-inch baking pan with nonstick cooking spray, being careful not to coat sides of pan.

2. In a medium saucepan, melt butter; remove from heat. Stir in granulated sugar, the water, and vanilla. Stir in flour, cocoa powder, and baking powder until combined. Stir in chocolate pieces. Pour batter into prepared pan.

3. Bake for 15 to 18 minutes or until a toothpick inserted near the center comes out clean. Cool on a wire rack. Remove from pan. Cut into 16 bars. Sprinkle with powdered sugar.

Per brownie: 103 cal., 4 g total fat (2 g sat. fat), 8 mg chol., 56 mg sodium, 16 g carbo., 0 g fiber, 1 g pro.

Strawberries with Lemon Cream

A few snips of lemon basil top this refreshing dessert. If you can't find lemon basil, use plain basil and sprinkle on a pinch more finely shredded lemon peel.

Start to finish: 10 minutes
Makes 6 servings

- 3 cups halved fresh strawberries
- 1 cup whipping cream
- 2 tablespoons powdered sugar
- ⅛ teaspoon ground cardamom
- ¼ teaspoon finely shredded lemon peel
- 1 tablespoon snipped fresh lemon basil or basil

1. Divide berries among six dessert dishes; set aside.

2. In a chilled medium bowl, combine whipping cream, powdered sugar, and cardamom. Beat with an electric mixer on medium speed until soft peaks form (tips curl). Fold in lemon peel.

3. Spoon whipped cream mixture over berries in dessert dishes. Sprinkle individual servings with snipped basil.

Per serving: 168 cal., 15 g total fat (9 g sat. fat), 55 mg chol., 16 mg sodium, 8 g carb., 2 g fiber, 1 g pro.

Cook Out Tonight

Impress guests or family with quick-fixing yet elegant endings to backyard cookouts. Strawberries with Lemon Cream (above), Caramel Clementines (page 176), and Fill-the-Grill Nectarine Toss (page 176) are all terrific choices. Keep the rest of the menu easy by serving burgers, steaks, or chops with a tossed salad and corn on the cob or baked potatoes.

Quick Apple Crisp

In this simple version of an all-time favorite, granola subs for the traditional crumb topping.

Start to finish: 15 minutes
Makes 4 servings

- 1 21-ounce can apple pie filling
- ¼ cup dried cranberries
- ¼ teaspoon ground ginger or ground cinnamon
- ¼ teaspoon vanilla
- 1 cup granola
- 1 pint vanilla ice cream

1. In a medium saucepan, combine pie filling, dried cranberries, and ginger; heat through, stirring occasionally. Remove from heat; stir in vanilla. Spoon into bowls. Top individual servings with granola. Serve with ice cream.

Per serving: 507 cal., 15 g total fat (8 g sat. fat), 68 mg chol., 113 mg sodium, 88 g carb., 6 g fiber, 9 g pro.

Peach Shakes

You can whirl this enchanting fruit shake together in a flash, so keep the ingredients on hand for any time you want a treat.

Start to finish: 10 minutes
Makes 3 (about 10-ounce) servings

- 2 cups frozen unsweetened peach slices
- 1¾ cups milk
- 1 to 2 tablespoons honey
- 1 teaspoon vanilla

1. In a blender, combine frozen peach slices, milk, honey, and vanilla. Cover and blend until smooth. Pour into glasses.

Per serving: 145 cal., 3 g total fat (2 g sat. fat), 11 mg chol., 72 mg sodium, 25 g carb., 2 g fiber, 5 g pro.